Immigration and Contemporary British Theater

POSTCOLONIAL STUDIES

Maria C. Zamora
General Editor

Vol. 13

This book is a volume in a Peter Lang monograph series.
Every title is peer reviewed and meets
the highest quality standards for content and production.

PETER LANG
New York • Washington, D.C./Baltimore • Bern
Frankfurt • Berlin • Brussels • Vienna • Oxford

VICTORIA SAMS

Immigration and Contemporary British Theater

Finding a Home on the Stage

PETER LANG
New York • Washington, D.C./Baltimore • Bern
Frankfurt • Berlin • Brussels • Vienna • Oxford

Library of Congress Cataloging-in-Publication Data

Sams, Victoria.
Immigration and contemporary British theater:
finding a home on the stage / Victoria Sams.
p. cm. — (Postcolonial studies; v. 13)
Includes bibliographical references and index.
1. Theater—Great Britain—History—20th century. 2. Theater—
Social aspects—Great Britain. 3. Ethnic theater—Great Britain—History—20th century.
4. Ethnicity in the theater. 5. English drama—20th century—History and
criticism. 6. Emigration and immigration in literature.
7. Immigrants in literature. I. Title.
PN2595.S245   792.0941—dc23   2011053456
ISBN 978-1-4331-1305-5 (hardcover)
ISBN 978-1-4539-0590-6 (e-book)
ISSN 1942-6100

Bibliographic information published by **Die Deutsche Nationalbibliothek**.
Die Deutsche Nationalbibliothek lists this publication in the "Deutsche
Nationalbibliografie"; detailed bibliographic data is available
on the Internet at http://dnb.d-nb.de/.

Cover illustration "The Arrival" Copyright Jane Laurie 2013
www.janelaurie.com

The paper in this book meets the guidelines for permanence and durability
of the Committee on Production Guidelines for Book Longevity
of the Council of Library Resources.

Printed in Germany

Contents

Acknowledgments

To those who have made me feel at home wherever I am in the world, I owe an unfathomable debt, especially to my famously vast extended family, who truly make me savor life. I am particularly grateful for my brother and sister, and for the family they have added to ours. My mother's compassion, curiosity, and encouragement are a source of strength and an example to me. I hold the memories of my father's humor, insight, and humility close to my heart, and miss him more than I can say.

Much love and gratitude go out to the longtime friends who have sustained my spirits across any distance: Mike and Vicky Callen, The Oakleys, Clovis and the much-missed Hala Maksoud, Aida and Roy Karaoglan, Alexandra Ossipoff, Kathleen Cedergren, Tris Anne DeSalvio, Marisa Nightingale, Tiffany Smink, Marina Moskowitz, Eric Steadman, Tiffany Holmes, Maia Mulligan Kaz, Laura Kreutzer, Judy Kramer, Samantha Levy and Jason Deutsch, Reggie Tindall, Suze Fowle, Jenny Backus, Laura and Bob Foose, Anna Lürbke, Alexi Daher, Paola Moscarelli, Lloys Frates, Kris Over, Tammy Ho, Kelly Jeong, Matt Christensen, Antonia Couling-Dini, and Robert Sargant. I am also deeply grateful for the friendships formed a mere "kick of the ball" from my door in Carlisle with the likes of Pauline Cullen and Brian McKenzie, Ebru Kongar and Mark Price, Cotten and Clare Seiler, Becky and Dave Richeson, Heather and Vince Champion, Rachel Boggia, Lucile Duperron and Marc Mastrangelo, Suzanne and Dave Kranz, Emily Lawrence, and Andy and Circe MacDonald. Amy and Alex Bates, Ashley Finley, Rennie Mapp and Rafael Alvarado, Francesca Amendolia and Ed Webb, and Sarah Skaggs all made life on Pomfret even sweeter.

Huge thanks go out to the mentors and comrades who have taught me so much about intellectual excitement and community: to the teachers who first taught me how to research and write (Ellis Turner and Bob Thomason); to my guide through the deepest waters of comparative literature (Emily Apter); to the wisest of advisors on dissertations, academic survival, and so much more (Jenny Sharpe); and to my research group mates at Dickinson College—led by the fabulous and inimitable Sharon O'Brien—Peggy Frohlich, Elizabeth Lee, Patty van Leeuwaarde Moonsammy, Jerry Philogene, Regina Sweeney, Andy MacDonald, and Antje Pfannkuchen. Another dear friend and colleague, Amy Wlodarski, deserves thanks for her insight and encouragement on my writing.

The best parts of this book are indebted to the knowledge and generosity of the scholars and artists whose work has inspired and aided mine: Sarah Dadswell, Giovanna Buonanno, Christiane Schlote, Jatinder Verma, Kristine Landon-Smith, Dominic Hingorani, Dimple Godiwala, Valerie Kaneko-Lucas, Mustapha Matura, Felix Cross, and Nicolas Kent. Thanks also to all the theater companies and to the R&D Committee of Dickinson College for providing me the means to pore over production files and travel to conferences. I had several wonderful homes away from home in London during many research trips, for which I am deeply grateful to my family and friends who are family. I am thankful as well for the sharp eyes and thoughtfulness of my dearest readers: Bill Truettner, Alison Steadman, Pauline Cullen, Ann-Lloyd Hufstader, and Lisa Sams. Jackie Pavlovic and Heidi Burns at Peter Lang deserve hearty thanks.

For another important form of sustenance that fuelled the writing of this book, I thank Naomi and Robert Pham (and their lovely children) for all the Issei deliciousness.

For all they did to sustain me in stomach and spirit, and for all they taught me about immigrating to a faraway country with courage and style and a sense of humor, I thank and miss my Sittou Hajar and Sittou Adele always.

A final note of profound gratitude for the friendship and example of a remarkable mentor, teacher, and translator: Michael Henry Heim, who has left the door open to so many beautiful literary worlds.

Illustration/Photo Credits

The image on the front cover of the book is by illustrator Jane Laurie and was commissioned for Tamasha Theatre Company's 2013 adaptation of Shaun Tan's *The Arrival*. The photograph on p. 53 in Chapter Four is from the program for Tamasha Theatre Company's 1996 production of Ayub Khan-Din's *East is East*. The photograph on p. 84 in Chapter Five shows the London home of Tara Arts, and was provided by its Artistic Director, Jatinder Verma.

Timeline

500

| IMMIGRATION HISTORY | Immigration has been a formative influence on British demography from earliest historical records—the 5th and 6th centuries show 50,000 to 100,000 Angles and Saxons migrating to the island from Northern Germany and Denmark, giving England its name. The only inhabitants at the time were Britons, also known as Celts. |

1100

| IMMIGRATION HISTORY | After the Angles, Saxons, Danes, and Norse, Normans arrived and settled mostly in Southern England. |

1243

| IMMIGRATION HISTORY | Passage of a statute that made it legal to expel Irish beggars from England. |

1290

| IMMIGRATION HISTORY | Expulsion of Jewish inhabitants of England—10,000 approximately; Jews were not allowed back until the mid-1600s, when Cromwell is said to have allowed a significant number of Jewish migrants entry into the country. They formed the bases of communities for later immigration of the 19th and 20th centuries. |

1596

| IMMIGRATION HISTORY | The Immigrants Act by Queen Elizabeth I is passed, prohibiting entry into England of any black persons and mandating the expulsion of those living in England at the time. |

1771

| IMMIGRATION HISTORY | Ban on slaveholding within Britain. By the eighteenth century, 10–15,000 blacks had settled in Britain (adding to those who remained in spite of the expulsion edict of 1596). |

1815

| IMMIGRATION HISTORY | The start of a period (1815–1945) that saw a net immigrant population growth of 1.5–2 million, in a total population that grew from over 20 million in 1850 to nearly 50 million in 1950. Most of these immigrants were from elsewhere in Europe. One million were Irish. |

1921

| POLITICAL EVENTS | Ireland gains its independence from Britain on December 6. |

1945

| IMMIGRATION HISTORY | 150,000 exiled Polish army, government, and dependents allowed to settle in Britain. |

1947

| POLITICAL EVENTS | India, Nepal and Bhutan gain independence from Britain. |

1948

| IMMIGRATION HISTORY | • British Nationality Act: Allows entry to Britain of Empire and Commonwealth citizens.

• Empire Windrush sails from Jamaica to Tilbury Docks with 417 passengers. |
| POLITICAL EVENTS | • Riots against Blacks in Liverpool and Indians in Birmingham.

• Ceylon gains independence from Britain and becomes Sri Lanka.

• Burma gains independence from Britain. |

1953

THEATER HISTORY	First season of Theatre Workshop, at Theatre Royal Stratford East in London.
POLITICAL EVENTS	Coronation of Queen Elizabeth II.

1954

POLITICAL EVENTS	Egypt gains independence from Britain.

1956

THEATER HISTORY	English Stage Company established at Royal Court Theatre; Berliner Ensemble (Brecht's company) visits London. John Osborne's *Look Back in Anger* premieres at Royal Court in May.
POLITICAL EVENTS	• Sudan gains independence from Britain. • Nasser nationalizes the Suez Canal; France and Britain begin intervention, then withdraw from Port Said without reclaiming Suez. Crisis leads to PM Anthony Eden's resignation in early 1957.

1958

THEATER HISTORY	• Errol John's Trinidad-set *Moon on a Rainbow Shawl* comes to Royal Court Theatre from the United States (play had been written in 1953). • Jamaican-born Barry Reckord's *Della (Flesh to a Tiger)* produced at Royal Court Theatre • Theatre Workshop premiere of Shelagh Delaney's *A Taste of Honey*. •Harold Pinter's *The Room* premieres.
POLITICAL EVENTS	Riots against West Indians in Nottingham and Notting Hill.

1959

THEATER HISTORY	Arnold Wesker's *The Kitchen,* set among immigrant and native British workers in a London restaurant kitchen, premieres at the Royal Court Theatre.
POLITICAL EVENTS	Stabbing murder of Antiguan-born Kelso Cochrane by a group of white youths at Notting Hill Carnival. Compared to Stephen Lawrence murder for police mishandling of investigation and dismissal of racial motive, in spite of fascist activity in the area.

1960

THEATER HISTORY	Barry Reckord's *You in Your Small Corner,* about an interracial love affair, opens at Cheltenham Theatre, and then the Royal Court Theatre.
POLITICAL EVENTS	Nigeria and Cyprus gain independence from Britain.

1961

THEATER HISTORY	Tom Murphy's *A Whistle in the Dark*, about Irish migrants to Coventry, produced by Theatre Workshop at the Theatre Royal Stratford East.
POLITICAL EVENTS	British Cameroons, Tanganikya and Zanzibar (now The Republic of Tanzania), Kuwait, and Transvaal gain independence from Britain.

1962

THEATER HISTORY	Founding of the National Theatre, which becomes the Royal National Theatre with a permanent home on the South Bank by 1975.
IMMIGRATION HISTORY	Commonwealth Immigrants Act: restricting entry into Britain of foreign nationals from Commonwealth into Britain. Bill marks first formal distinction between those born in Great Britain and those born outside it.
POLITICAL EVENTS	Jamaica, Uganda, and Trinidad and Tobago gain independence from Britain.

1963

POLITICAL EVENTS	Swaziland gains independence from Britain.

1964

POLITICAL EVENTS	Malta gains independence from Britain.

1965

POLITICAL EVENTS	• Race Relations Act: establishment of Race Relations Board and grievance procedures for employment, housing, and other forms of discrimination based on race. • Singapore gains independence from Britain.

1966

POLITICAL EVENTS	Barbados and British Guiana gain independence from Britain.

1967

POLITICAL EVENTS	Establishment of National Front.

1968

THEATER HISTORY	Theatres Act dissolves censorship powers of Lord Chamberlain (ending over two hundred years of censorship over all plays seeking license for public performance in Britain).
IMMIGRATION HISTORY	Commonwealth Immigrants Act: Further restricting entry of Asians and Africans with British passports.
POLITICAL EVENTS	Race Relations Act: establishment of Community Relations Commission.

1969

THEATER HISTORY	• Dark and Light Theatre Company founded by Frank Cousins and based in Longfield Hall—Brixton, though largely a touring company due to Arts Council funding restrictions. It closed down in 1975, when it was renamed (and redirected) as the Black Theatre of Brixton, run for its brief afterlife by Norman Beaton, Ali, and Rufus Collins (see 1975). • Tom Murphy's *Famine* comes to the Royal Court Theatre.

1970

THEATER HISTORY	• Keskidee Arts Centre founded by Oscar Abrams, a former architect from Guyana, who came to Britain after working in Tanzania. The center was based in Islington and became a safe space and dynamic educational and artistic force for social change within the community—offering courses and after-school programs for children and youths, as well as producing original theater and revivals. It remained active even as it faced financial challenges and ultimately lost its funding from the Arts Council in the late 1980s, eventually closing in 1992. (Chambers, 146–148) • Mustapha Matura's *Black Pieces* (three short plays about immigrant and Black British Londoners) premieres at Institute of Contemporary Arts, London.

1971

THEATER HISTORY	Mustapha Matura's *As Time Goes By,* about a young Trinidadian couple in West London, premieres at Traverse Theatre, Edinburgh.
IMMIGRATION HISTORY	Immigration Act: Consolidates previous acts and tightens some restrictions on new immigrant entry and family reunification.

1972

THEATER HISTORY	• Temba Theatre Company founded in London by Alton Kumalo and Oscar James, and then directed by Alby James from 1984 to 1990. • Foco Novo founded in London by Roland Rees, David Aukin, and Bernard Pomerance. Produced work by Alfred Fagon, Mustapha Matura, Howard Brenton. •Alfred Fagon's *11 Josephine House*, about Caribbean migrants in Bristol, produced by Foco Novo at Almost Free Theatre.
IMMIGRATION HISTORY	Expulsion of Asians from Uganda who were not Ugandan citizens (approximately 60,000 people), 27,000 of whom are admitted into Britain.

1973

THEATER HISTORY	Michael Abbensetts' *Sweet Talk*, about the troubled marriage of young Caribbean migrants, opens at the Royal Court Theatre.

1974

THEATER HISTORY	• Drum Arts Centre founded by Cy Grant (from Guyana, RAF veteran and POW of WWII) and John Mapondera "to create a national arts organization." Drum produced numerous plays and workshops at venues throughout London (ICA, King's Head) before changing leadership for a final season at Riverside Studios in 1979 under new artistic director John Burgess. (Chambers, 151–153) http://www.cygrant.com/about2.html
	• Alfred Fagon's *No Soldiers in St. Paul's,* about young first-generation Caribbean immigrants, opens at Metro Club Theatre in Notting Hill, London.
IMMIGRATION HISTORY	Attacks upon Irish targets in Birmingham following pub bombings by IRA in the city.
POLITICAL EVENTS	Prevention of Terrorism Act: Allows for detention and interrogation of suspected terrorists (effectively any Irish person, by passport or appearance) for up to seven days. http://cain.ulst.ac.uk/hmso/pta1974.htm

1975

THEATER HISTORY	• Black Theatre of Brixton formed out of demise of Dark and Light Theatre. Run by Norman Beaton, Ali, and Rufus Collins, the company produced many acclaimed productions in myriad venues (after losing its building) from the Roundhouse to Beaton's restaurant, the Green Banana. (Chambers 142–144).
	• Alfred Fagon's *Death of a Black Man* premieres at the Hampstead Theatre, London.

1976

THEATER HISTORY	• Tara Arts Theatre Company founded by Jatinder Verma, Sunil Saggar, Ovais Kadri, Vijay Shaunak, and Perveen Bahl, and based in London.
	• Naseem Khan publishes *The Arts Britain Ignores.*
POLITICAL EVENTS	Race Relations Act: Establishes Commission for Racial Equality.

1977

THEATER HISTORY	Mary O'Malley's *Once a Catholic*, set among second-generation immigrant schoolgirls in a convent school in London in 1956, premieres at the Royal Court Theatre.

1978

THEATER HISTORY	Mary O'Malley's *Look Out...Here Comes Trouble!* is produced by the RSC at the Warehouse Donmar Theatre in London.
POLITICAL EVENTS	Dominica gains independence from Britain.

1979

THEATER HISTORY	Black Theatre Co-Operative founded by Mustapha Matura and Charlie Hansen. Their first production is Matura's play about second-generation immigrant youths, *Welcome Home, Jacko*, performed at the Factory and then at Riverside Studios, Hammersmith, London. Theatre in London.
POLITICAL EVENTS	St. Lucia and St. Vincent gain independence from Britain.

1980

THEATER HISTORY	• Caryl Phillips' *Strange Fruit*, about a Caribbean immigrant mother and the tensions with her two sons, produced at the Crucible Theatre in Sheffield. • Michael Abbensetts' *Samba*, set in a mini-cab office, produced at Tricycle Theatre, Kilburn, London. • Howard Brenton's *The Romans in Britain*, imperialism from Roman invasion to British in Northern Ireland. •Tunde Ikoli's *Scrape off the Black* premieres at Riverside Studios, Hammersmith, London (and is revived in 1998 at Theatre Royal Stratford East, London).
POLITICAL EVENTS	• Southern Rhodesia (now Zimbabwe) gains independence from Britain. • Riots in largely Caribbean St. Paul's area of Bristol.

1981

THEATER HISTORY	Hanif Kureishi's *Borderline*, set in Southall, London in the run-up to an actual BNP march there that triggered violence, is produced by Joint Stock Theatre Company. The company interviewed first- and second-generation Asian residents of Southall as well as other residents and community organizers, and then converted the interviews into a play through a workshop with actors. The play was performed at the Royal Court Theatre.
IMMIGRATION HISTORY	Nationality Act: Indirectly restricts entry of non-white Commonwealth and Empire citizens through the patrilineal British birth requirement.
POLITICAL EVENTS	• Antigua and Barbuda gain independence from Britain. • Inner city riots in multiple locations throughout Britain, with widespread allegations of police brutality and racial profiling, as well as racially-motivated violence by others against residents of the affected areas (Brixton, Liverpool, London). • Publication of the Scarman Report on the Brixton riots (documenting arbitrary and often repressive police tactics and public mistrust of law enforcement institutions)

1982

THEATER HISTORY	• Theatre of Black Women co-founded by Patricia Hilaire, Paulette Randall, and Bernadine Evaristo. • Caryl Phillips' *Where There Is Darkness,* an expressionist drama about a middle-aged Caribbean immigrant on the eve of his return to Jamaica, is produced at the Lyric Theatre Hammersmith. •Edgar White's *Man and Soul,* about two immigrant men in a London detention centre, is produced by Black Theatre Co-Operative at Riverside Studios, Hammersmith.

1983

THEATER HISTORY	Edgar White's The Nine Night and Ritual by Water are produced together at the Factory, London. The first play focuses on the intergenerational tensions in a Jamaican immigrant family, and the second is set among different generations in a youth center in Hackney.

1984

| THEATER HISTORY | •Alby James becomes Artistic Director of Temba Theatre Company. |
| | •Edgar White's *The Boot Dance* is produced by Temba at the Tricycle Theatre, London. |

1985

| THEATER HISTORY | • Talawa Theatre Company cofounded by Yvonne Brewster, Carmen Monroe, Mona Hammond, and Inigo Espejel in London. |
| | • Nigel Moffat's *Mamma Decemba*, about an older immigrant widow, is produced by Temba Theatre Company at Birmingham Repertory Theatre. |

1986

THEATER HISTORY	• Double Edge Theatre Company founded by Amani Naphtali in London.
	• Karim Al-Rawi's *A Colder Climate*, set in Hackney and dramatizing the relationships amongst a Black British youth perpetually seen as an immigrant, an Arab-British girl, and their friends and family members.
	• Tunde Ikole adapts Gorky's *The Lower Depths* to an immigrant family in the East End for the Tricycle Theatre in Kilburn, London.

1989

| THEATER HISTORY | • Tamasha Theatre Company cofounded by Kristine Landon-Smith and Sudha Bhuchar. |
| | • Harwant Bains' *Blood* premieres at the Royal Court Theatre Upstairs. |

1990

| THEATER HISTORY | • Kali Theatre Company cofounded by actress Rita Wolf and playwright Rukhsana Ahmad to produce new writing for theater by women of Asian background. Their first production, Rukhsana Ahmed's *Song for a Sanctuary*, dramatized the lives of immigrant and second-generation South Asians in a women's shelter in London. |
| | • Jatinder Verma directs his adaptation of *Tartuffe* at the National Theatre, making him the first Asian director to work at the National. |

1991

| THEATER HISTORY | • Mustapha Matura's *The Coup* is first play by Caribbean playwright to be produced at National Theatre.

• Jatinder Verma directs Shakuntala's *The Little Clay Cart*, first Asian play to be produced at National Theatre. |

1992

| THEATER HISTORY | Paul Boakye's *Boy with Beer,* featuring second-generation Caribbean and African immigrants' experiences in Britain, premieres at the Man in the Moon Theatre, London. |

1993

THEATER HISTORY	Trish Cooke's *Running Dream,* dramatizing three generations of a family split between Dominica and England, is produced by Theatre Royal Stratford East.
IMMIGRATION HISTORY	Asylum and Immigration Appeals Act restricts inflow of immigrants by enabling the detention and reducing the benefit entitlements of asylum seekers while they are awaiting decisions on their cases.
POLITICAL EVENTS	Stabbing murder of Stephen Lawrence, the eighteen-year-old son of Jamaican immigrants, by five white youths at a bus stop in South London.

1995

| THEATER HISTORY | • Ruth Carter's *A Yearning,* an adaptation of Federico Garcia Lorca's *Yerma* set within an Asian immigrant household in Birmingham.

• Anne Devlin's *After Easter,* is produced by the RSC at The Other Place, Stratford-upon-Avon. The play follows the visions experienced by an immigrant from Northern Ireland who has been living in England for many years. The visions trigger a breakdown and seem to "call her home" to Belfast.

• Winsome Pinnock's *Leavetaking* is produced by National Theatre. First Black British play to be produced at National. |

1996

| THEATER HISTORY | Ayub Khan-Din's debut play, *East Is East,* a co-production of Tamasha Theatre Company, Birmingham Repertory Theatre and the Royal Court Theatre, premieres at Birmingham Repertory Theatre. |

1997

THEATER HISTORY	Parv Bancil's *Crazyhorse* premieres at the Old Vic, Bristol (collaboration between Tara Arts and Paines Plough).

1998

THEATER HISTORY	Sol B. River's *48/98*, a fantastical vision of a London museum of the future—with the exhibit being a Jamaican immigrant family home—is produced by Talawa Theatre Company at the Lyric Studio Hammersmith.

1999

THEATER HISTORY	Richard Norton-Taylor's *The Colour of Justice* presents the Stephen Lawrence investigation and trial through what becomes the Tricycle Theatre's signature approach to documentary theater: verbatim drama. The play goes on to a sell-out national tour and a television broadcast that draws one of the largest viewing audiences of British television history.

2000

THEATER HISTORY	• Tamasha Theatre company produces *Balti Kings,* co-written by Sudha Bhuchar and Shaheen Khan at the Birmingham Repertory Theatre. The play follows the drama within the kitchen of a family-owned Birmingham Balti restaurant from the perspectives of its staff. • Philippe Cherbonnier's *58,* produced by Yellow Earth Theatre Company and inspired by the discovery in Dover of 58 suffocated stowaway migrants on a cargo truck from Belgium, is produced at Gardner Arts Centre in Brighton (and then Soho Theatre in London). • Tanika Gupta's *The Waiting Room* premieres at the National Theatre, and is the first play by a British Asian playwright to be produced at the National.

2001

THEATER HISTORY	• Timberlake Wertenbaker's *Credible Witness,* a dramatization of interwoven refugee stories, is produced at the Royal Court Theatre. • Jimmy Murphy's *The Kings of the Kilburn High Road* comes to the Tricycle Theatre, London.

2002

| THEATER HISTORY | • Roy Williams' *Sing Yer Heart out for the Lads* premieres at the National Theatre. |

2003

| THEATER HISTORY | • Kwame Kwei-Armeh's *Elmina's Kitchen*, an intergenerational immigrant drama set in a Hackney café, is produced by the National Theatre.

• Tanika Gupta adapts Harold Brighouse's Victorian drama *Hobson's Choice* to an Indian migrant family in Lancashire, and it opens at the Young Vic in London.

• *Strictly Dandia*, a Tamasha production co-written by its artistic directors, it dramatizes the comic and poignant conflicts that arise between differing generations and religions within Glasgow's Asian community. The play, set at a series of dance competitions, premiered at the Edinburgh Theatre Festival, transferred to the Lyric Theatre Hammersmith, and then toured the UK.

• Nadim Sawalha's one-man show, *All I Want Is a British Passport*, chronicles the challenges facing one of Britain's most famous immigrants, Mohammed Al-Fayed. The show is produced by Tamasha Theatre Company and opens at the Actors Centre, London. |

2004

| THEATER HISTORY | • Gurpreet Kaur Bhatti's *Behzti* premieres at the Birmingham Repertory Theatre company, closing shortly after its opening after threats from individuals and groups offended by its treatment of taboo subjects. The play takes its audience from the home of a Sikh immigrant woman and her adult daughter to the temple where their relationships to each other and their fellow Sikhs are tested by a series of traumatic experiences.

• Kwame Kwei-Armah's *Fix Up* premieres at the National Theatre.

• Phillippe Cherbonnier's *58* is produced by the Yellow Earth Theatre Company at Gardner Arts Centre in Brighton. The play's title and story are drawn from the discovery in Dover in 2000 of fifty-eight suffocated Chinese stowaways on a cargo truck from Belgium. |

2005

THEATER HISTORY	• Tanika Gupta's *Gladiator Games,* which dramatizes the story of Zahid Mubarak, a young British Asian man murdered by his cell mate while detained for a petty crime. The killing, which took place in Feltham prison in 2000, was found to be racially motivated.
	• Tamasha's *The Trouble with Asian Men* (created from 160 interviews with Asian men), premieres at the Arts Depot and Soho Theatre in London.
	• Sonja Linden's *Crocodile Seeking Refuge* is produced by her Ice and Fire Theatre Company at Lyric Theatre Hammersmith.

2007

THEATER HISTORY	• Clare Bayley's *The Container,* set within a truck carrying illegal immigrants to England, premiered at the Edinburgh Theatre Festival. The play is performed within an actual container truck converted into a theater space.
	• Enda Walsh's *The Walworth Farce,* a production of the Galway-based Druid Theatre Company opens at the Traverse Theatre, Edinburgh, as part of the Festival. The play is a slice-of-life on repeat as an Irish immigrant father and his two sons reenact their day of departure from Ireland as scripted, directed, and judged by the father.
	• Ayub Khan-Din's adaptation of the Bill Naughton play *All in Good Time* opens at the National Theatre. Khan-Din sets his adaptation in the Bolton home of an Indian immigrant family and titles it *Rafta, Rafta.*

2008

THEATER HISTORY	• Em Hussain makes her playwriting debut with *Sweet Cider,* a co-production of Tamasha Theatre Company and Arcola Theatre, London. Two British-Pakistani girls run away to an Asian refuge in northern England.
	• Fin Kennedy's *Unstated: Stories of Refuge* is an interview-based play produced by Red Room Theatre Company at Southwark Theatre, London.
	• Rukhsana Ahmad's *Letting Go* is produced with Oladipo Agboluaje's *For One Night Only* by Pursued By a Bear at Oval House Theatre, London. The plays feature as a double bill dramatizing experiences of contemporary refugees seeking asylum in Britain.
	• *Suspended Lives,* a co-production of Change of Frame and IPSA at Tara Arts theatre in Earlsfield, South London, stages the experiences of asylum seekers.

2009

THEATER HISTORY	• Richard Bean's *England People Very Nice,* a play-within-a-play that farcically presents a history of immigration to Britain from the 1500s to the present, premieres at the National Theatre.
	• Oladipo Agboluaje's *The Hounding of David Oluwale,* an adaptation of Kester Aspden's account of the murder investigation of a homeless immigrant killed in 1969, premieres at the West York.
	• Tara Arts and Hanif Kureishi adapt Kureishi's novel, *The Black Album,* into a play by the same name, which premieres at the National Theatre.

2010

| THEATER HISTORY | Linda Brogan and Polly Teale's *Speechless,* based on Marjorie Wallace's book *The Silent Twins,* is produced by Shared Experience at the Edinburgh Fringe Festival. It begins a national tour from Oxford in September 2011. |

Introduction

To let. A valuable site at the cross-roads of the world. At present on offer to European clients. Out-lying portions of the estate already disposed of to sitting tenants. Of some historical and period interest. Some alterations and improvements necessary.

— Alan Bennett, *Forty Years On*

After more than a half-century of post-war devastation and reconstruction, recession, and recovery, and even prosperity, Britain's major cities, especially London, entered this millennium as cosmopolitan centers. They were no longer the direct beneficiaries of imperial expansion and colonial enterprise but have continued to draw immigrants seeking economic or political refuge in a relatively prosperous and politically stable Western Europe. These cities have been forced to redefine themselves under new conditions and within an interdependent regional and global economy. As a post-imperial metropolitan capital, London in particular acts as the center of new versions of national identity for an England and a Great Britain poised between Europe, the United States, and elsewhere. While the flow of migrants and capital has been most heavily concentrated in London, it directly involves multiple locations within and beyond London as well, within a landscape of powerful local ties and complex regional and transnational affiliations. Furthermore, devolution has helped to make these locations the centers of newly imagined communities. Cities such as Liverpool, Glasgow, Manchester, and Leicester have generated active "glocal" economies and cultural production and contain their own long histories of migration as well.

As the epigraph above suggests, the metaphorical link between domestic spaces and national identity resonates powerfully in British culture. The collective investment in Britishness is often acutely focused in two areas: its theatrical heritage and its housing. From Shakespeare to Bennett, and from Windsor Castle and 10 Downing Street to Richard Hoggart's working-class row houses in Leeds, Britain's self-image draws heavily on the cultural capital of its playwrights and theaters, as well as on what James Procter calls its "dwelling spaces." The late writer Quentin Crisp gave a satirical twist to these connections by wryly and frequently declaring himself "England's Stately Homo." In his memoir, *The Naked Civil Servant,* Crisp simultaneously mocked and celebrated the icons and monuments of a Britain that excluded and criminalized homosexuality during his youth.[1] Ambivalence about British (and English) nationalism and such investment in cultural patrimony is not unique to Crisp; indeed, such ambivalence features heavily in postwar British cultural production and commentary from the new wave films of Lindsay Anderson to the opinion pages of *The Guardian.* Theatrical examples abound, whether the unease that suffuses Harold Pinter's *Homecoming* or runs through the grander spaces of Alan Ayckbourn's *House & Garden.*

While theater vies with ever more forms of cultural production for public attention in Great Britain, it still remains more deeply tied to Britain's collective vision of its heritage than film, visual arts, or other art forms. Theatrical history and landmarks are studiously tracked and preserved, and London has long proclaimed itself the "Theatre Capital of the World." Tourism and marketing slogans should not necessarily be taken at face value (or perhaps should *only* be taken at face value), yet they do suggest the constitutive role that theater and domestic space have played in England's national self-image. The buildings that house British theater such as the Haymarkets or Empires or Theatre Royals suggest an anchoring or "homing" of theater in tension with its ephemeral and nomadic qualities. The very names of these theaters suggest forms of movement more commonly associated with Britain, namely that of commerce, exploration, imperial expansion, and travel. Through its analysis of the staging and repercussions of immigration on contemporary British theater, this book aims to illustrate how migrants' experiences of home and location, historical memory and nostalgia, belonging and alienation, profoundly inform these national identities. While its title might seem to refer exclusively to individual immigrants seeking and "finding a home," it also addresses the ways Britain has been figured as a home, and how it might do so anew through its drama and its theaters.

The subject of this book derives from a lifelong preoccupation with migration, perceptions of place and feeling "at home." Home is a term both familiar and elusive, or even contested, one that conjures many emotions and thoughts while very likely carrying different significances for each person.[2] Witold Rybczynski describes home as a space of the imagination and of invented tradition.[3] Madan Sarup further illustrates this multiplicity of meaning:

> We speak of *homecoming.* This is not the usual, everyday return, it is an arrival that is significant because it is after a long absence, or an arduous or heroic journey. If some food is home-made, it connotes something cooked individually or in small batches. It is

not something mass-produced, it is nutritious, unadulterated, wholesome. [...] We also say, 'it is time you were told some *home truths*'. These are truths about one's character or one's behavior that are unpleasant and perhaps hurtful, and which can be expressed only in a caring environment, where people are concerned about you.[4]

Sarup's observations illustrate the associations commonly made between "home" and familiarity, privacy, comfort, trust, and intimacy. Home consists of something other than physical materials and built space, something close to but not exactly like communal identity. When we speak of a "home away from home," it often signifies a place in which we do not feel the estrangement we might when distant from the place that we would call our home.

What do we take for granted when we imagine home as a fixed or stable place? As Doreen Massey puts it, "That place called home was never an unmediated experience." Is displacement or dislocation an aberration or is it the defining condition of human life? If so, how do we explain or respond to the apparent need to find or make a place called home? In the introduction to *Homemaking: Women Writers and the Politics and Poetics of Home*, editors Catherine Wiley and Fiona Barnes argue that "Living as we do now, in a world where new nations emerge from the collapse [and the often powerful remnants and resurrections] of old political structures, the idea of home as a starting point and a returning haven becomes ever more attractive and yet paradoxically more difficult to attain."[5] The newness of such volatility and of global migration is widely invoked, but worth examining more closely for its assumptions about historical and contemporary conditions. In her questioning of the rhetoric around globalization and its conditions of "spatial upheaval," Massey incisively notes the reliance of such rhetoric on the premise of an original stability and security: "Those who worry about a sense of disorientation and a loss of control must have felt they knew exactly where they were, and that they had control."[6] She goes on to question the newness of such upheaval for those whose worlds have been shaped by invasion, conquest, or simply by vast disparities of power and access to resources. Some migrants might view their departure from the source country as a precious opportunity or even a welcome adventure, a move that they meet with eager anticipation but not without anxiety. Stuart Hall reads such a mix of emotions in the photographs of arrivals from the Caribbean to the London rail stations, photographs that appeared in local papers in the 1950s and 1960s, seeing in the "expectant look" towards their future and their new location, as suggesting "the dead end of one thing and the uncertain beginning of another."[7]

Chapter One

FINDING A HOME
ON THE STAGE

What, then, does "home" mean with respect to post-imperial Britain and its inhabitants' relationships to spaces and places beyond its borders? Rajagopalan Radhakrishnan puts the question differently in his study of diaspora and globalization, stating that the "challenging and complex question is how to enable a mutually accountable dialogue among the many locations that have something important to say about the 'after' of postcoloniality."[1] For colonial and post-imperial migrants to Britain, disorientation and dislocation may well be a constitutive condition of the place from which they migrated, whether colony or newly-independent nation. Such conditions often (particularly for colonial migrants from the Caribbean) combine with an uncanny sense of familiarity with the "mother" country to which they are migrating. In a speech given in London in 1995, Trinidadian-born Pearl Connor recalls that the Caribbean migrants of her generation "knew more about England and the British than the British knew of them."[2]

In the title essay of his collection *Imaginary Homelands*, Salman Rushdie asserts that an Indian emigrant writer's identity is "at once plural and partial," that by virtue of the duality (or plurality) of cultures that is part of the colonial legacy for India, all its emigrant or exile writers may be "haunted by some sense of loss, some urge to reclaim."[3] Perhaps all postcolonial emigrant writers share in this plural and partial identity, as a condition of the simultaneously divided and hybrid cultural terrain that is part of the colonial legacy, and a condition of migration and adaptation to a new location. Dramatists and poets such as

Derek Walcott and Seamus Heaney offer their own variations on this sense of fragmentation and multiplicity and its implications for their writing. Homi Bhabha argues that ambivalence plays a constitutive role in the constructions of individual "national subjects," as well as in the understanding and articulation of "nation-spaces" and their political and cultural collectivities.[4] Bhabha focuses primarily on the ambivalences that he locates at the core of European national self-images (in his treatment, mainly England and France) with respect to their identifications of a racial "Other" embodied by their colonial subjects and located within their colonial territories.

This book revises Bhabha's formulation of the establishment of the "cultural boundaries of nation" through the "ambivalent, antagonistic perspective of nation as narration" by examining how such perspectives might be narrated, staged and transformed in British drama and theater.[5] What the plays and productions treated here reveal is how these ambivalent constructions of national and communal spaces and identities are further complicated not only by the fusions and fissures within a multicultural English national "self," but also by those within these "homes" in Britain and those imagined or left behind in the source countries. Bhabha's "ambivalent, antagonistic perspective" bears out in the ways in which Britain's former colonies appear in these productions as "other" nation-spaces to an assumed imperial center, while its immigrant and minority homes similarly figure as "others" within a racially or culturally proscribed nation-space. The plays discussed here, however, shift these "other" homes and figures from the edges of these national narratives to center stage. Theater calls attention to this performativity of national history and identity by self-consciously establishing its boundaries, its center and margin (or wings), its spaces as settings, and its time as duration. This happens both on and off the stage: a theater's location often conveys both geographical and social significances. Sometimes the social significance trumps the geographical, such as when one finds the Royal Shakespeare Company's Stratford-upon-Avon theaters in the West End listings, and the Bridewell Theatre (located in the center of London) in the Fringe listings. Sometimes theaters can be responsive to their own setting, as in the case of the Tricycle Theatre or the Leicester Haymarket, whose work reflects cultural affinities or partnerships with its local immigrant and minority populations. Such an interpretation informs this book's perpetual confrontation with the ways in which, in a world of widespread dislocations prompted by privilege and deprivation, one's sense of home and belonging can find its echoes, its challenges, and even its transformation in theater (as text, as experience. or as place).

In his reflections on our relationship to places and to pasts, Rushdie suggests ways in which memory and migration might work on our imaginations, both individually and collectively. The lingering passage from his essay defines meaning as "…a shaky edifice we build out of scraps, dogmas, childhood injuries, newspaper articles, chance remarks, old films, small victories, people hated, people loved…" or the psychological raw materials that we carry.[6] Out of these unstable raw materials we might also build the larger structures of our identities and our sense of connection to places and people; in other words, the means by which we make ourselves at home in a place (or feel alienated from it). Doreen Massey argues that social relations are what define place and home for us.[7] While home may be intimate, personal and subjective, it is not necessarily the private domain envisioned in the dominant bourgeois concept of domesticity. Thus, it may be collectively inhabited or imagined, and as such, functions as "the site of a sometimes uneasy coalition between personal space and community life," according to Catherine Wiley and Fiona Barnes.[8]

In the introductory essay from the catalogue for an exhibition entitled "No Place (Like Home)," held at the Walker Arts Center in Minneapolis, museum director Kathy Halbreich's approach to the concept of "home" and its relationship to history is helpful:

> In its most traditional definition, it is designated as a refuge or a place of origin. "Home" is not a physical thing made of bricks and mortar… It is what defines, and, in some cases, justifies…what we are. "Home" is constructed on the foundation of that which we come from and that to which we aspire.[9]

Whether they construct it as a fantastical (sometimes ironic) alternative or as a more attainable reality, the theater artists treated in this book enact Rushdie's "simultaneously plural and partial" perspectives in their constructions of home. The first chapter examines two of the prevailing narratives about immigration to Britain, narratives with complex and long political and cultural roots. The plays and theater history discussed throughout the book are all deeply connected to these narratives, in some cases explicitly and directly echoing or debating them.

The second chapter of the book addresses the process of emigration and the staging of the conditions that drove emigration and those that awaited those migrants that arrived in Britain. The plays examined here often contrast the perspectives of immigrants long settled in the UK with those of their younger selves, revealing the expectations that they carried with them and the ways their host country met (or frustrated or surpassed) those expectations. The subsequent chapter focuses on dramatizations of the challenges facing immigrants with families, and of the tensions that emerge both within and between differing generations. What emerges in these plays are the ways that racism and patriarchal oppression fuel each other, presenting challenges for immigrants that can have traumatic and even violent consequences. This chapter examines the implications such challenges have for male migrants in particular, while the chapter that follows addresses the challenges faced by migrant and diasporic women in Britain, as characters and as theater artists. It places its analysis of recurring motifs within plays about women from adolescent to elderly in the context of the landscape of theatrical production and scholarship, and the work by and about women within this landscape. Each of these chapters emphasizes the ways in which that theater has presented diverse visions of home, and shows how the artists and characters have worked to find or create homes for themselves within their communities and theatrical spaces. In addition, the book traces the popular and critical uses of the term "visibility" and "visible minorities" and its connotations of exposure or display to analyze how these plays depict the consequences as well as the empowering potential of visibility. Each chapter explores how the plays stage the filtering of postwar and post-imperial Britain into these domestic spaces and the characters' absorption of and response to their repercussions. They also explore how the plays' productions and the artists involved make their own incursions into the cultural space and history of post-war Britain.

A Note on Terms

Home is not the only term with fluid and subjective meanings used in this book. Both colonial legacies and postwar identity politics have combined to make various terms of identity fraught with occasionally conflicting connotations. The term "Black," for instance, has been a designation with roots in colonial hierarchies of race that link darkness of skin with genetic and biological inferiority. The identity category of "Black British," while it links to this racialist history, has also been embraced as a tactical and coalitional identity linking ethnic minorities subjected to and resisting discrimination and persecution in Britain. "Black" as an identity category can also be used to link those born in Britain with those from the Caribbean, Africa, and Asia. In the 1970s and 1980s, "Black British" often included people of Asian and Arab background, and prior to that also Greek Cypriots and Maltese. While anti-racist movements still retain some of these alliances, many groups and individuals self-identify along more ethnically, religiously, or regionally specific lines (e.g., Pakistani, Sikh, Hindu, Caribbean, African, Rastafarian, Muslim).[10] The term "Asian" in British usage typically refers to the subcontinent of South Asia (Pakistan, India, Bangladesh, and Sri Lanka), with "East Asian" referring to Southeast Asia and the Pacific islands. The term "minority" is fraught for those "visible" and "invisible" groups, as discussed in Chapter Two. The term often connotes non-white British-born ethnic groups, and in official reports often excludes such ethnic minorities as Irish or Polish.

In some usage (such as Mary Karen Dahl's study of Black British theatre), "postcolonial" embraces all artists of African diasporic background, both British-born and immigrant, in an effort to establish the historical conditions that produced a long-standing, non-immigrant Black presence in Britain and to combat the assumption that all black theater in Britain is immigrant theater.[11] For the purposes of analyzing the colonial legacies of the largest immigrant and ethnic minority groups within Great Britain (Irish, Caribbean, and South Asian), the term "postcolonial" here includes immigrants from these three regions and their descendants. This term is often used to describe the latter two groups, but largely excludes the Irish from such consideration. Though this book's focus is on immigration as subject of and historical context for the plays it treats, it does take up second-generation immigrant writers and issues, particularly when discussing intergenerational relationships and challenges. It differs from Dahl and others' exclusive focus on Black British or British Asian artists and work as the lens through which to read the afterlife of imperial racism in contemporary Britain. It does so by taking a comparative postcolonial approach to Irish diasporic experiences and their dramatic representations, which seem to have received more attention in the social sciences than in the humanities.

Along with diasporic theatrical influences on postwar Britain and the stories it tells about itself, devolution has played an increasingly visible role in reshaping the narratives of British identity. The national narratives of Scotland and Wales as well as those of regional and local identities within England have grown more inclusive of black British and British Asian writers and stories, acknowledging the ways in which diasporic influences are not restricted to metropolitan culture and institutions. The works in focus in this book link their stagings of domestic spaces to these regional and national narratives of British identity and to various concepts of home and belonging for postcolonial diasporic subjects in Britain. The book does not, however, succeed in doing for British theater history what James Procter seeks to produce in *Dwelling Places:*

Postwar Black British Writing, "… an increasingly differentiated, *devolved,* cultural geography of black Britain over the past fifty years."[12] Most of the theater companies and productions here discussed are based in London, even as plays might be set elsewhere in Britain. This metropolitan focus corresponds to a concentration of theatrical resources and institutions in London, but it would be remiss not to acknowledge the complex history and significance of the theatrical activity and historiographical work that has emerged from other urban centers and towns in the UK. The hope is that this work will add to the larger project of excavation and comparative analysis underway.

Chapter Two

NARRATIVES OF IMMIGRATION AND THEATER IN POSTWAR BRITAIN

Dueling Perceptions of Immigration

In a recent survey, over 40% of the UK population polled rated immigration the most pressing issue for contemporary British society, and those polled overestimated the numbers of immigrants entering the UK annually by at least two to three times the actual rates.[1] This contention over the impact of immigration is not restricted to recent years. Debates over what "British culture" means and the ways that factors such as immigration might enrich or threaten it date back centuries, but the rise of television and radio (and more recently, the Internet) certainly seems to have amplified and accelerated their reach. Such perceptions have implications for theater artists who create work about immigration to Britain, as well as for where and how those immigrants and minorities living in Britain make their home. Contemporary theater artists seem to be increasingly active participants in the public discourse addressing immigration as a historical and as a contemporary phenomenon. Some of their commentary and their dramatic work echoes the perceptions described above, and some, consciously or not, contradicts them. Much of their work is based on the assumption that British culture, however that may be defined, has been profoundly influenced by its experiences as a host country to immigrants. In this sense, the emergence of more diverse domestic settings on the British stage in the postwar period can be read as signaling new and possibly competing visions of Britain's domestic and global identities. The ways that home has come to be defined on stages throughout Britain—both those homes represented within the plays and those homes sustained through theaters' venue design, audience and artist involvement, and community building—ties closely to the changing networks and dynamics linking British residents and sites to people and places elsewhere in the world.

Historian Tony Judt claims that the impact of World War Two and of the Suez Crisis upon Britain transformed its national image from an expansive imperial power to a diminished player in a world political scene dominated by the United States. He argues that the "first lesson of Suez was that Britain could no longer maintain a global colonial presence," particularly after its military and political supremacy had been thrown into doubt already by its reliance upon its allies and its colonial subjects during World War Two.[2] Echoing postwar scholars of film and theater such as Stephen Lacey and Samantha Lay, Judt contrasts the confidence of the early postwar "new Elizabethan Age," which he characterizes as marked by the 1953 coronation of Queen Elizabeth and the climbing of Everest by a British team in that same year, with the national mood following the devastating impact in 1956 of both the invasion of Hungary by the Soviets and the Suez Crisis.[3] Judt goes on to discuss how Britain's national decline was economic as well as political and symbolic, particularly with respect to its economic ties to the Commonwealth countries.[4]

These changes were accompanied by longer term demographic shifts in the British population due to internal and external migration. From the beginning of the twentieth century to the early 1940s, Britain was sending out more migrants than it was taking in. By the start of postwar reconstruction, this emigration coupled with British war casualties had produced internal labor shortages that drove the government and private enterprise to recruit migrants to work in transportation, nursing, manufacturing, and the building trades, among other areas.[5] They turned to Ireland and to the colonies in the Caribbean and those in Asia, where they could draw a skilled labor force from the civilian population as well as from those colonial subjects who had served in the war effort. After the war, the 1948 British Nationality Act was passed, which redefined all those born in Britain and its colonies as British citizens, and eased the processes of labor recruitment from the colonies. The Ireland Act of 1949 accompanied Irish withdrawal from the Commonwealth in 1949, and extended the same rights of citizenship to the Irish, deeming them British subjects as they were declaring themselves to be an independent republic. Thus, between 1948 and 1962, "Britain's [immigration regulations] rested on the assumption of free entry and settlement for British subjects throughout the world."[6] These shifts were accompanied by a boost in the birthrates, such that from 1950 to 1970, the UK population rose 13%. This population growth was less dramatic than that happening across Europe, where countries like The Netherlands (35%), Sweden (29%), France (30%) and West Germany (28%) saw surging birth and migration rates and declining infant mortality rates in this period.[7]

From the early postwar period to the early 1960s, the rates of immigration from the Caribbean and South Asia were low, with about 16,000 people from the Caribbean and 3,000 migrants from India arriving each year. Beginning with the 1962 Commonwealth Immigration Act, stricter limitations were placed on the numbers of British overseas citizens, particularly on the mainly non-white "New Commonwealth" citizens, allowed to settle in the UK. Susan J. Smith cites as factors the recession that hit the British car industry that year and the simultaneous application of Britain to join the European Economic Community, whose common labor market viewed Britain's importation of "New Commonwealth" migrant labor as a threat.[8] By 1976, the total number of "nonwhites" in the UK population was approximately 1.85 million (3% of the total UK population), and 40% of this group was born in the UK.[9]

The growth of the population of Caribbean, South Asian, and African background from 1940 to 1990 was slightly more dramatic, rising from a fraction of 1% in 1940 to close to 6% in 1990, according to Ian R. G. Spencer, whose account of British immigration policy from 1939 to the present argues broadly that governmental immigration policies both shaped and responded to public attitudes about immigration, national community, and race.[10] Spencer's identification of popular and governmental concerns and of the framing of British immigration policy underscores the persistent characterization of non-white immigration to Britain as an unprecedented and potentially threatening phenomenon.

In spite of the passage of the relatively progressive Race Relations Act of 1965, which established limited protections for immigrants and minorities against housing and employment discrimination, the middle to late 1960s marked a consolidation of popular support behind the increasingly racist rhetoric and policies of Enoch Powell, a Conservative MP from

Wolverhampton. Judt points out that one result of the 1965 act is that "English landladies could no longer display signs announcing 'No Blacks, Irish, or Dogs,'" acknowledging a practice alluded to frequently in fictional and nonfictional accounts of the climate that greeted postwar migrants to the UK. While immigrants and minorities were gaining minimal legal protections, Powell's political speeches during these years—most notably his infamous 1968 "Rivers of Blood" speech—presented incendiary images of an England besieged with waves of immigrants, and of a society in which "the stranger, the disgruntled, and the *agent provocateur*" are empowered against the "native-born worker" (images that Conservative Party leader and Prime Minister Margaret Thatcher later echoes in her descriptions of English culture and landscape being "swamped" with immigrants).[11] His argument that prevention of immigration and repatriation were necessary for England's survival made him both a highly popular and a highly controversial figure. Powell's rhetoric proved to be too inflammatory for many of his fellow party members, and ultimately led to his being banned from Conservative Party leader Ted Heath's shadow cabinet.[12] In 1968 and 1971, further legislation was passed that revoked "...an earlier agreement to admit Ugandan Asians with British passports," and that placed further limitations on the admission of British citizens without family origin in the UK (a patriality clause that was a thinly disguised means of restricting non-white immigration from British colonies and Commonwealth nations).[13] The trend of further immigration restrictions continued through the 1970s and into the 1980s, when the levels of immigration hit their twenty-year low.

What are the roots of this gap between popular perception and demographic reality, and what does it mean to be a visible immigrant or minority in contemporary Britain? This persistent gap has prompted closer analysis by scholars in contemporary migration studies. Mary Hickman argues that much of the "analyses produced about the impact of and responses to the immigration of people from the Indian subcontinent and the Caribbean in the 1950–70s have emphasized 'newness', new racism, new political discourses, new fears of an 'enemy within.'"[14] This narrative of the newness of an immigrant presence in or of unprecedented "waves" of immigrants to Britain reinforces characterizations of earlier immigrants as more culturally similar to the British and more readily assimilable to the British "way of life," or what Hickman calls the "myth of [pre-World War Two British] cultural homogeneity."[15] Paul Gilroy locates a similar myth at work in the political rhetoric linking immigration to Britain's failing economy and weakening global position: "The process of national decline is presented as coinciding with the dilution of once homogenous and continuous national stock by alien strains."[16] Even in celebrations of a culturally heterogeneous Britain, one often finds this emphasis on "newness" and on discontinuity with its past, as with Panikos Panayi's positive reading of the impact of postwar immigration on British society:

> Few other social developments in the history of Britain since the end of the Second World War have had the same impact as immigration. The millions of newcomers who have made their way to the islands off the north-western coast of Europe since 1945 have helped to transform them into the more vibrant, multi-ethnic, colourful state that is Britain today. What would Britain look like without the post-war newcomers? Everybody would basically be white. There would be greater dress conformity. England would have less success in sporting competitions. Sections of the inner cities would find themselves in a worse state than the one currently existing, as immigrants have transformed many of them. English diet would remain rather bland.[17]

Panayi's claim, with its emphasis upon the visible and physical (and culinary) signs of difference, echoes the rhetoric of immigration that ties "newness" and "foreignness" to skin color and physical attributes as firmly as it does to cultural practices. Panayi's praise for what he defines as the benefits of immigration belies the complexity of his own work in immigration history, work that has highlighted the ways in which Irish, Germans, Portuguese, and other immigrants who were defined as racial others in earlier periods have been absorbed and homogenized into a "British" culture against which these "newcomers" have been defined.[18] Why is the "impact" of immigration so widely perceived as a postwar phenomenon?

Britain has long shuttled between a cultural insularity and an expansiveness that absorbs and reshapes diverse cultural and linguistic influences, many of which have been the by-products of its imperial expansion and colonial rule. In spite of the prevalence of this rhetoric of "newness," the stories that Britain tells about its demographic and cultural history are varied and often contradictory. The accounts and representations of migration and the formation (and now devolution) of Great Britain have largely taken two paths: one narrative corresponds to the aforementioned "myth of cultural homogeneity" and the other narrative traces a long history of immigration and its constitutive cultural influences throughout Britain, but especially in London.

Floods and Waves and Rivers, Oh My!

This first narrative of British immigration history generally describes the postwar period as featuring unprecedented levels of immigration into the UK that have altered British society in entirely new ways. Many of these examinations of postwar British history characterize the UK as suddenly becoming "an immigrant society" set against a long history of low rates of immigration and of immigrants who assimilated uneventfully into English and then British culture.[19] This vision of postwar change finds symbolic reinforcement in the depictions of new immigrants to Britain increasingly found in literature, radio, film, advertising, and to a lesser degree, in theater of the postwar period.

Frequently accompanying this narrative are recurring metaphors of British places and culture being flooded, "swamped," overrun, or inundated by immigrants and their influences, or of "waves" of migrants bringing new customs, foods and more with them. Whether denounced as a threat or positively invoked in such accounts, these new patterns of immigration are said to be profoundly reshaping Britain in unprecedented ways.[20] The ambivalence of this narrative emerges in the representations of the ways "the British diet" has been altered by a growing population of immigrants and by the importation of foods from other regions of the world, whether cheering such changes as Panayi does or decrying the rising popularity of curry as a challenge to fish and chips as national dish. Such profound influences date back to the introduction of tea and coffee centuries earlier. Plays such as Arnold Wesker's *The Kitchen* and Tamasha Theatre Company's more recent *Balti Kings* portray the restaurant landscapes of cities like London, Manchester, and Birmingham as reflective of the more recent population displacements across Europe and Asia in World War Two and in numerous violent conflicts and wars since. Both plays depict British restaurant kitchens as the center stage settings within which these refugees and economic migrants introduce "new" flavors and cooking methods to an invisible public (in both cases figured as ethnically English and located offstage). In so doing, these plays make service employees visible subjects while at the same time depicting the native-born customers as invisible objects.

Many of the celebrations of the fiftieth anniversary of the 1948 arrival to England of the *Empire Windrush* feature versions of this narrative, citing this embarkation as presaging a "new" multiculturalism in Britain. Though it was neither the first nor the only ship to bring Caribbean migrants to the UK after World War Two, and brought fewer than 500 migrants from Jamaica to a country of over fifty million inhabitants, this ship's arrival is frequently invoked as a milestone of British immigration history, and Caribbean migrants of this period are often referred to as the "*Windrush* generation." The *Windrush* was a captured Nazi troop ship that had been renovated by the British and was already carrying sixty Polish passengers picked up in Mexico when it arrived in

Jamaica. In Jamaica, the ship picked up an additional 430 Caribbean migrants (not all of them were Jamaican), many of them skilled workers already employed by the armed forces or with jobs arranged prior to their departure.[21] The numbers of immigrants to the UK from the Caribbean were in the hundreds per year at this time, climbing to the thousands in subsequent years, but never hitting the levels one might imagine from the rhetoric surrounding their entry into Britain.[22] David Ellis, Peter Fryer, and others put the total number of Caribbean migrants between 1948 and 1953 at between five and six thousand, adding to a population of between fifty and sixty thousand of Caribbean descent.[23] By 1966, this population had grown to a total of 454,100 from the Caribbean and 50,700 West Africans.[24] The docking of the *Windrush*, nevertheless, was one of the most highly anticipated and publicized arrivals to England, giving its name to an entire generation of postwar migrants whose images and stories have featured in countless forms since that date. Newspapers and newsreels documented the experiences of such notable passengers as the calypsonian Aldwyn "Lord Kitchener" Roberts ("London is de place for me") as well as the reactions to the ship's arrival.[25] In the fiftieth anniversary year of the voyage, the writers Trevor and Mike Phillips published an oral history of these migrants' experiences, titled *Windrush: The Irresistible Rise of Multi-Racial Britain*, and in the sixtieth anniversary year, the Imperial War Museum created a special exhibition, *From War to Windrush*, documenting the personal stories of West Indians during the two world wars, from their direct involvement on the frontlines to the experiences of those who remained in the Caribbean, and those who migrated to Britain after the end of the war.[26] The arrival of this ship and its Caribbean passengers symbolizes for many a watershed transformation of British society.[27]

The British Bulldog Is a Mutt

The alternate narrative that has captured the public imagination is caricatured by Richard Bean in his 2009 play *England People Very Nice*, which had a commercially successful run on the National Theatre's main stage, if a critically and popularly combative reception.[28] With its cavalcade of immigrant characters from the past centuries, the play presents a comic vision of contemporary immigration to the UK as merely the latest link in a chain of immigrant arrivals and settlement in Britain dating back to the Middle Ages. One of the first signals that the play walks a line between crude stereotypes and a parody of crude stereotypes is Bean's play title, which mimics the speech of an immigrant with limited English language skills.

While Bean mocks the speech, perspectives, and cultural stereotypes of a chain of immigrants to Britain from 1500 to the present, Robert Winder sarcastically echoes anti-immigrant rhetoric by titling his history of immigration to Britain during the same period *Bloody Foreigners*. After a catalogue of the cultural and botanical immigrants to Britain (from the Christian religion to leeks and nasturtiums), Winder counters the Britain-is-being-swamped vision with an emphasis on the unacknowledged history of human immigration to Britain, arguing that

> …the rhetoric that seeks to depict modern immigration into Britain as a hazard, putting at risk a thousand-year way of life, plays false with historical truth: Britain has always accommodated strangers. One of the reasons why it has been able to absorb so many overseas citizens in recent times is that people have been settling here since time began. Immigration is an old, old story, one that defines the texture of British life every bit as significantly as our grand heritage of stately homes—many of which themselves have immigrant foundations.[29]

Winder's and Bean's narratives of accommodation and absorption build on earlier accounts such as the satirical poem "The True-Born Englishman" first published by Daniel Defoe in 1701.[30] In fact, the opening song of Bean's play, "A True-Born Londoner," is a riff on Defoe's poem, and like the poem, the play contains numerous caricatures and cultural stereotypes. The poem's most commonly repeated lines (cited by Winder as well as by many others), "Thus from a mixture of all kinds began, / That heterogeneous thing, an Englishman," follow Defoe's mock-chronicle of wars, religious persecution, invasions, and other push or pull factors that have made the English "pedigree" a mixture of Pict to Norman to Turkish. Defoe intercuts his satire with more earnest declarations about the benefits for England of welcoming and absorbing the finest qualities of "foreign" cultures, "For as the Scots, as learned men have said, / Throughout the world their wand'ring seed have spread, / So open-handed England, 'tis believed, / Has all the gleanings of the world received."[31]

Defoe's celebration of England as a cultural mutt finds a more recent champion in the late Robin Cook. In a 2001 speech to the Social Market Foundation, Cook (serving as foreign secretary at the time) offers his own debunking of the myth of cultural homogeneity:

> The British are not a race, but a gathering of countless different races and communities, the vast majority of which were not indigenous to these islands. [...] The idea that

Britain was a pure Anglo-Saxon society before the arrival of communities from the Caribbean, Asia, and Africa is fantasy.[32]

Throughout his speech but particularly in the above remarks, Cook explicitly challenges purist invocations of a "British way of life" and national culture, and the (not always) implicit xenophobia and racism that accompany them. Playwright Clare Bayley takes a similar view in the preface to her play, *The Container*, which followed an earlier play she had written about a Kurdish refugee in London. Bayley explains:

Immigration has long been an integral part of our country's make-up, and never more so than now. Yet despite this…the story of what people have come from, what they have gone through to get here, and what they are confronted with when they do arrive—is largely ignored.[33]

Bayley's plays take a decidedly different approach from Bean's. An immediately obvious difference is in the characterization, which, as her quote above suggests, aims to give a fuller dimension to migrant stories that are often decontextualized or caricatured. Bean's characterization depicts its migrants through broad cultural stereotypes, which simultaneously drew praise from some critics and theatergoers for its irreverent mockery of all cultures treated and accusations of racist caricature by some of its critics and audience members. [34] Rather than distancing the audience from the action of the play through proscenium staging and a play-within-a-play structure, Bayley's approach is to try to align the audience and character as closely as possible through the physical setting of the play and through immersion in the dialogue between the characters. Both playwrights, however, share this view of immigration to Britain as a long-standing formative influence on its culture.

Narratives and Numbers

How then do these dueling narratives connect to the demographic impact of immigration? According to the 2001 Census, ethnic minorities constituted 4.5 million, or 7.6% of the total population of the UK. In London, this percentage climbs to 29%, while in Scotland and Wales, ethnic minorities constitute 2% of the population.[35] While popular perception seems largely to favor the *Windrush*-and-waves version of British history, Bean and Winder and Cook's visions of a historically heterogenous England (or Britain) correspond much more closely to recent scholarship on immigrant settlement in regions and cities such as London, Liverpool, and Yorkshire, as well as that on British cultural and social history. What accounts for these perceptions, then, as well as for the prevailing ideas that the British cultural landscape is more profoundly marked by immigration in this period than ever before. Is it the presence of greater numbers of "visible minorities" in British cities and towns? Could it be tied to new technologies of global communication and transportation and the ways in which they have redrawn the local and global maps? Is it the cumulative impact of centuries/generations of migrants?

A 1993 Museum of London exhibition titled *The Peopling of London* sought "…to counter the assumption that London has experienced extensive immigration only since the end of the Second World War."[36] In its companion book, many contributors note the dearth of integrated scholarship on immigration to London and to Britain more broadly, and argue that this neglect has misrepresented the constitutive roles that immigrants and immigration have played in the past and present of both London and Great Britain. The book features essays by contributors such as Rozina Visram and Colin Holmes, whose work on immigration and immigrant communities has gained traction as more of the traces of these histories are being acknowledged and preserved.

Sukhdev Sandhu's gracefully told stories of London's Black and Asian residents and writers from the 1500s to the twenty-first century argue persuasively for their formative influences upon London's metropolitan culture. In his introduction, he too takes issue with the "newness" of this presence, remarking that "Popular culture encourages the conflation between London, ethnicity, and newness…None of this is heinous, but neither, except in terms of scale, is it especially new."[37] In his analysis of legal cases concerning the rights of immigrants and second-generation immigrants, Jacob Selway argues that in the sixteenth and seventeenth centuries: "Immigration from beyond the British Isles, not just incipient empire, shaped national identity. Early modern multiculturalism played a crucial role in the development of Englishness."[38] Theater companies such as Talawa and Tara (more fully described later in this chapter) engage in a postcolonial dramaturgy that illuminates this role through their "tradaptations" (or transformative adaptations) of classical European drama and through devised theatrical productions.[39] Their theatrical projects have added to a growing body of excavatory historical and dramatic work that makes unseen connections and presences visible. Such work complicates the relationships that these narratives have established between national community, place, and rootedness.

Going back still further, documents from the fifth and sixth centuries suggest the earliest migrants to the British Isles were the 50,000 to 100,000 Angles and Saxons who sailed from Northern Germany and Denmark, giving

England its name. The only inhabitants of the islands at the time were the Britons (whom the Celts displaced). With the arrival of the Normans in the twelfth century, there was more traffic between the continent and the British Isles, bringing more European migrants into the country. The absorption of these migrants was never wholly free from violent xenophobia, as evidenced by the expulsion in 1290 of the approximately 10,000 Jewish people living in the country at the time. Many sources argue that Elizabeth I's 1596 proclamation calling for the expulsion of all 'blackamoors' from England is one indication of an early African presence in England at this time. Panikos Panayi notes that "small groups of immigrants and refugees trickled in between 1066 and 1815," but he argues elsewhere in the same book that larger numbers of immigrants from France, Africa, and the Caribbean moved to Britain in the seventeenth and eighteenth centuries.[40] Sukdhev Sandhu estimates that the number of blacks in eighteenth-century England was no more than 10,000, while Panayi's study puts this number at between 10,000 and 15,000 of a total population of close to ten million.[41] Sukhdev Sandhu notes that even in the 1700s, "the notion (however insecurely founded in reality) that too many black people were entering the country animated a number of critics," whose anxieties might have also been heightened by the circulation of images of black people used in advertising and appearing in the work of artists of the period (William Hogarth being a notable example).[42]

Most estimates put the total number of immigrants to Britain from 1815 to 1945 at close to two million, with the overall population starting at under twenty million and rising to close to fifty million by the later date. The largest immigrant population in the nineteenth and twentieth centuries came from Ireland, followed by smaller numbers of German and Russian immigrants.[43] In stark contrast to contemporary popular narratives of earlier immigrants as more assimilationist, Panayi describes the immigrants of that period as largely settling in urban centers and as making "efforts to maintain their ethnicity against the encroachments of the dominant grouping."[44] Furthermore, Panayi challenges the notion that anti-immigrant sentiment is a new phenomenon by describing how the popular discourse of the past centuries referred to immigrants as arriving in waves and constituting a threat to the dominant culture.[45] Anti-immigrant sentiment went beyond the verbal with attacks on Italian and German businesses and persons and with the wartime internment of Germans from the beginning to the middle of the twentieth century.

Proximity to the British Isles, along with an earlier start to colonization may have contributed to Ireland's role as source of the largest number of immigrants to Britain for centuries. Their recorded presence could be said to date to 1288, with the first documented murder in Fleet Street, and centuries later and more happily, with London's first Irish mayor.[46] Colin Holmes argues that Irish women constituted a largely overlooked migrant group (in historical studies). Many of them worked in textile mills, domestic service, and laundries.[47] For the period from 1541 to 1800 when Ireland was ruled as a "subordinate kingdom" and then from 1801 to 1922, when the Act of Union brought it under British rule, migration from Ireland was treated officially as internal migration. The peak years of Irish emigration were the largely famine-driven decades in the mid-1800s, and then the years from 1920 to 1950, when the Irish economy was ailing and Britain surpassed the United States as the primary destination for Irish migrants.[48] While annual immigration has risen and fallen, Irish immigrants and their descendants have for many decades formed the largest minority group in the UK.

Rozina Visram notes that the majority of South Asian settlers in Britain from the late eighteenth through the nineteenth centuries were single male sailors (lascars), nannies (ayahs) and other domestic servants. Many of the male Asians in London married white women, which was "generally frowned upon and was the subject of much negative comment, as lascars were viewed with contempt."[49] During the nineteenth century, the abolition of slavery and the expansion of the British Empire and its infrastructure prompted the recruitment of Asian labor to other British colonies in Africa and the Caribbean, a practice that continued until 1917.[50] Such work was termed "indentured" but in practice was often indistinguishable from slavery, although some of these workers eventually obtained their freedom and settled in the new countries.[51] These workers were later joined by voluntary immigrants who may have been their family members or workers and merchants seeking greater opportunities abroad.[52] In the latter part of the nineteenth and early twentieth centuries, a small number of Asian lawyers, businessmen, and academics arrived in Britain, becoming actively involved in causes from Indian nationalism to women's suffrage to local and national British causes.[53] After World War One, labor shortages in the UK drew mainly Sikh migrants to work in factories and mills in London and other cities.[54] The partitioning of India and Pakistan in the run-up to Independence provoked the migration of over eight million people in the region, with roughly four million Muslims migrating into Pakistan, and just over that number moving from Pakistan into India.[55] Dilip Hiro argues that these conditions of subcontinental migration, coupled with the social segregation of British and Indians that underpinned its colonial administration, meant that far fewer Indians than Caribbean colonial subjects viewed Britain as their "mother country."[56] Further, Hiro cites the immigration laws in India as critical factors in the relatively low numbers of Indian and Pakistani migrants to Britain up to 1960, and then in the rise in numbers from 1960 onward, when it reached the levels of Caribbean immigration at that time.[57] At their peak rates of migration, the Asians and Caribbeans that arrived in Britain each year numbered in the tens of thousands, respectively. By 1991, the total population of South Asian migrants (from India, Pakistan, and Bangladesh) in Britain was under 1.5 million, and the Caribbean and African migrant population was close to 730,000, out of a total population of 54,888,844 in Great Britain.[58] These numbers and the emerging histories of immigration suggest a more complex picture.

With respect to the reception of immigrants in past generations, Rozina Visram describes both benevolent activism and violence directed at the Asian population in London, the former with the opening of the Ayah's home in Aldgate in the 1870s and the Lascar Mission in 1887, and the latter with attacks on the Asian population in Canning Town in 1919, one incident in a broader national pattern of racially motivated violence in cities from Cardiff to Liverpool.[59] Growing Asian business communities in British cities that included restaurants, shops, religious institutions and cultural centers brought about new forms of Asian visibility. The early twentieth century saw the emergence of teashops and restaurants in London and, as chronicled in the program introduction to Tamasha Theatre Company's play *Balti Kings*, in other cities such as Birmingham and Manchester.[60] The first Indian-owned restaurant opened in 1927 in London, but the British had brought their own versions of curry (from "kari," a Tamil word for sauce) back with them from India as early as the eighteenth century.[61] By the 1940s, a Sikh temple (gurdwara) and the East London Mosque had been established to serve various religious constituencies of London, though no exact figures are available for the numbers of South Asian migrants in Britain until after World War Two. According to Amit Roy, there were ten Indian restaurants in the UK in 1955, growing to 1200 by the early 1970s, and to 7000 by 1991.[62] This gradual appearance of storefronts, restaurants, and cultural and religious centers in British cities signaled an increasingly established communal presence. Yet like Asian individuals and homes, these places were vulnerable to threats and racially motivated attacks.

It was the racially motivated murder of 16-year old Gurdeep Singh Chaggar in Southall on 4 June 1976 that inspired Jatinder Verma and three fellow university students to found the British Asian theater company Tara Arts in that year. In an interview with Graham Ley marking Tara's twentieth anniversary, Verma describes the murder as a catalytic incident, prompting him and many others to put their grief and anger into action.[63] Verma notes that Tara was the first British Asian theater group in Britain.[64] He goes on to describe their initial work as being driven by their desire to make their presence felt publicly in response to racist hostility and to the perceived absence of Asians from the stage and from the public sphere. [65] While Tara Arts' first production, Nobel Laureate Rabinadrath Tagore's *Sacrifice*, signaled the company's commitment to staging Indian drama (both ancient and modern classics), Tara's early repertoire also included newly devised work that dramatized the "double diasporic" experiences of those African-born Asians who, like Verma, had arrived in Britain in the late 1960s and early 1970s, by way of East Africa. Verma characterizes the group's early productions (following the Tagore play) as seeking to confront and illuminate the cross-cultural entanglements produced largely, but not exclusively, through imperial expansion and colonial rule. The company's expressed interest in exploring the histories and the implications of their members' presence in Britain has constituted both a political and an aesthetic practice.

Verma offers his views on how theater can reveal the contradictions embedded in such constructions of prior racial and cultural homogeneity:

> I began by observing that DNA suggests connected-ness. And wondering where in faiths, families, stories, moral values, we intersect. William Dalrymple's recent book, *White Mughals*, offers some startling facts in its footnotes. Up to the 1800s, one-in-three wills of Englishmen who'd been in India named the Indian bibi and the children he had borne with her as beneficiaries. By the 1830s, this figure slips to one-in-ten. After 1858, the names of Indian bibis or the children that ensued from any co-habitation with them simply disappear from wills. Another wilful attack of amnesia, but one which has profound consequences on our understanding of ourselves in modern England.[66]

His speech calls for an anamnesiac role for theater—one which provides its audiences with the context and connection lacking in the dominant narratives of immigration and policies of cultural promotion, literally mining the footnotes of historical studies to illuminate the undervalued or neglected connections. His emphasis on seeing and remembering links to his expressed concern with establishing alternate forms of visibility for Asians in Britain. In a 2001 speech at a conference held in Oldham, site of racially motivated violence and conflict between white and Asian youths and local police, Verma puts the issue to his audience, remarking: "This question [his speech title: 'Are We Visible?'"] seems to me to expose the paradox of 'visibility': we Asians are both 'visible' and 'invisible.' Our specificity is rarely presented in any public media, while our generality is increasingly apprehended."[67]

Many such attacks occurred in a climate of anti-immigrant hostility that often demonized all non-white people in Britain, immigrant and native-born alike. In the postwar period, this hostility was perhaps most famously articulated by a politician from the Midlands, the Conservative MP Enoch Powell, who, perhaps ironically, began his political career in the early 1960s advocating British recruitment of labor from the Caribbean. In his pivotal study of the discourse of race and nation in the UK, Paul Gilroy discusses the imagery in Powell's later speeches:

> This language of war and invasion is the clearest illustration of the way in which the discourses which together constitute 'race' direct attention to national boundaries, focusing attention on the entry and exit of blacks. The new racism [note how newness is emphasized in the official designation of the "New Commonwealth," where the white settler colonies comprise the unmodified or "old" Commonwealth] is primarily concerned with mechanisms of inclusion and exclusion.[68]

Powell's rhetoric, particularly in his "Rivers of Blood" gained him such notoriety that he became an iconic figure for anti-immigrant hostility, even a "monstrous figure in British politics," as the *Daily Telegraph* recently acknowledged in an article that urges a reassessment of Powell as an insightful and prescient politician on issues including but extending well beyond his views on immigration.[69] Nevertheless, Powell's language and his vision of the consequences of what he regarded as permissive immigration policies reveal a logic that translates colonial hierarchies of race into hierarchies of conditional citizenship that Gilroy argues

> …specifies who may legitimately belong to the national community and simultaneously advances reasons for the segregation or banishment of those whose "origin, sentiment, or citizenship" assigns them elsewhere. West Indians, for example, are seen as a bastard people occupying an indeterminate space between the Britishness which is their colonial legacy and an amorphous, ahistorical relationship with the dark continent and those parts of the world where they have been able to reconstitute it. Asians, on the other hand,…are understood to be bound by cultural and biological ties which merit the status of a fully formed, alternative national identity. They pose a threat to the British way of life by virtue of their strength and cohesion. For different reasons, both groups are judged to be incompatible with authentic forms of Englishness.[70]

Two of the most celebrated postwar British playwrights, John Osborne and Harold Pinter, implicitly question this vision in their earliest plays. Osborne's protagonist in his 1956 play *Look Back in Anger* asserts his working-class allegiances against what he views as a ruling-class mythology of national community. Jimmy Porter rails against this mythology and class from the confines of the cold-water flat in a Midlands city rooming house shared with his upper-class wife and their Welsh friend, who shares a market candy stall with Jimmy. The domestic setting of this play contains a microcosm of Britain's postwar, post-imperial internal conflicts. Harold Pinter's eerie first play, *The Room,* had its premiere in Bristol in 1957. Starkly dramatizing the perspectives on the outside world of the occupants of a one-room apartment in England, the play presents a critical take on an exclusionary nationalism, as staged entirely within the room of the play's title. Through its staging of a couple's varying responses to a series of visitors to the apartment, the play suggests the fears of displacement felt by those who lay claim to being insiders in England. For much of the play, these fears are expressed through the woman's fierce insistence on protecting her domain from the perceived threats or invasions of her visitors. Through oblique allusions to her past and to other rooms in the house, the woman's fate is linked to that of other people outside the room, particularly through Riley, a blind man described as "a Negro" in the stage directions, who brings her a message from her family. She reacts with anxiety, and then fear, suspicion, and denial at first, but ultimately she breaks down and touches the blind man's forehead and eyes. When her husband violently murders Riley, the woman immediately loses her sight and the play ends. The play suggests that nationalist invocations of "domestic order" deny the interconnected fates of insider and outsider, and mask the repressive violence sustaining such exclusionary fictions. The audience views these characters from the woman's perspective as they emerge into the room from an offstage outside world, and the play's treatment of blindness and revelation suggests further links between immigration, visibility, and vulnerability. Visibility, migration, and national community are themes picked up on by Tara Arts. Tara's response to the discourses critiqued by Gilroy involves a postcolonial aesthetic approach, or a dramaturgical version of the famous anti-racist slogan "we-are-here-because-you-were-there," that acknowledges and works from the contaminations of colonial history.

In the wake of two world wars, industrial and economic decline in Britain, decolonization in the Caribbean and elsewhere, and increased immigration from those former colonies into the U.K., this discourse of "nation" became, as Gilroy asserts, increasingly bound up with the discourses of "race" and of immigration. Gilroy argues that such exclusion from the imagined community

> ... is still felt today as black settlers and their British-born children are denied authentic national membership on the basis of their 'race' and, at the same time, prevented from

aligning themselves within the 'British race' on the grounds that their national allegiance inevitably lies elsewhere.[71]

During the 1980s, the boundaries of this national belonging were policed ever more vigilantly. This was done literally through the further tightening of controls on immigration into Britain and through the racialized definition and surveillance of "criminal elements" within an (allegedly) increasingly violent British society, as well as metaphorically through the "imagined community" of England or Britain. Gilroy argues, "the black presence is thus constructed as a problem or threat against which a homogenous, white, national 'we' could be unified."[72]

In the early postwar period, Irish immigrants and their descendants, ironically, had come to be identified (if somewhat precariously) with this "we." Kathleen Paul's research reveals that the official British government view of the Irish by 1948 linked them by virtue of 'blood' to the British, a connection made even clearer with the passage of the Commonwealth Immigration Act of 1962. This bill restricted rights of immigration for "New Commonwealth" citizens (again with the new!) while extending and encouraging Irish immigration:

> Using elements of the same rhetoric of blood, migration, and intermarriage as was employed for the emigrating children of the empire, the governing elite articulated its conviction that Irish and British nationals shared a common heritage and indeed were members of a common, if extended, family. Useful as a means of *including* the Irish, this reliance upon blood and race served also to *exclude* "Asiatic" nationals.[73]

Tom Murphy alludes to this conviction and the relative privilege it affords Irish migrants with respect to Asians. In his 1961 play *A Whistle in the Dark*, set in Coventry, one character says to a fellow Irish migrant, "One-way tickets back to the jungle for us too, Har [Harry], if they [the 'Muslims'] weren't here."[74] His remark suggests his understanding of the arbitrariness of race and of the ways in which Ireland and the Irish are seen as primitive. Immigration law would soon officially place the Irish in this ambivalent position within the hierarchy of British subjecthood. As Paul notes:

> By contending that Irish migrants should not be controlled, UK officials did more than argue for the retention of Irish citizens' rights of subjecthood. The larger debate revolved around a demographic hierarchy and the division of British subjecthood into groups with the right to enter the United Kingdom and groups without it. Contained within this debate was the question of how a nonsubject group, the Irish, could be allowed access to Britain....Thus, though perceived as a distinct community of Britishness, inferior to the domestic, Irish migrants apparently ranked higher than British subjects of color.[75]

What has not been widely acknowledged, however, is the way in which such privileging of the Irish in British rhetoric did not often translate into practice. Mary Hickman describes how, although Irish were privileged in some official policies and practices, they were also subject to disproportionate levels of arrest and deportation.[76] She goes on to argue that:

> The 'whiteness' of the Irish facilitated both continued access to their labour power for British employers, especially for the unskilled manual labour slot, and served to render them invisible within a reformulated British claim about the cultural homogeneity of the British Isles. It has enabled assumptions about the Irish to be made by innumerable writers about 'race' and ethnicity without any serious research evidence to back up their pronouncements about the ease of assimilation options faced by Irish migrants and their descendants compared with those who are visibly different. The article significantly ends by arguing that 'forced inclusion' within a national collectivity is no necessary protection against racialization, problematization and discrimination."[77]

In their 1997 report on discrimination towards Irish immigrants, Hickman and Bronwen Walter take this point further, arguing that the "racing" of Irish in policy and practice is more complex and contradictory, and that such discriminatory behavior has been at work in the scholarly, institutional, and popular treatment of the Irish in Britain.[78] Hickman argues in a later article that such treatment predated but certainly found renewed force in the passage of the Prevention of Terror Act in 1974, following the IRA-linked bombing of a pub in Birmingham:

> The evidence suggests that the use of the powers is targeted at two particular groups: principally young men living in Ireland and Irish people living in Britain. The legislation provides an examining officer (members of the Special Branch or Immigration and HM Customs and Excise officers) with the power to stop, and then examine, anyone who has arrived in or is seeking to leave Great Britain by ship or aircraft....According to one of the three official reviews of the Act (the Colville Report), there must be millions of examinations every year. The immigration control implications of the Prevention of Terrorism Act rarely intrude into the academic literature.[79]

The atmosphere for Irish in Britain in the 1970s and 1980s is widely described as tense, with heightened surveillance in public spaces and tightened scrutiny at immigration control, as well as attacks on Irish individuals and businesses. Hickman and Walter's report also notes the higher rates of illness, depression, and unemployment, as well as lower life expectancy rates for Irish in Britain, as compared with the general population.[80] The fluidity of the targets of discrimination and attack in Britain suggests both the arbitrariness of categories of race and ethnicity with respect to "British" identity, as well as their roots in colonial rule and domestic political expediency. Within such a context, then, in what ways have the arts responded to or participated in forming such constructions of national identity and of the "newness" of "New Commonwealth" immigration?

Prior to World War Two, several organizations and companies had been formed to support the diasporic communities in Britain and to promote Black intellectuals and artists and their work, such as the League of Coloured Peoples (1931) and the West African Students Union (1925), which both published magazines, as well as the activist Left and Unity Theatres and Robert Adams' wartime Negro Repertory Theatre.[81] In some ways, such activities provided them with a means of creating an alternative visibility to that imposed on them in their everyday lives. Literary depictions of these immigrants' lives appeared more widely in the 1950s, and mainly took the form of novels and short stories. Jeremy Poynting, founder of the Caribbean publisher Peepal Tree Press, describes the publishing opportunities for Caribbean writers of this period as overwhelmingly found in UK-based independent presses.

> The specific history of Caribbean publishing manifests very clearly the wider tendencies of global conglomeration in the trade. At the peak of the [1950 and 1960s] explosion of anglophone Caribbean fiction, with the exception of a handful of titles published by the Jamaican Pioneer Press, almost all of these (around 110 works of original Caribbean fiction) were published by no less than twenty-four different middle-sized literary publishers in the UK, such as Michael Joseph, Secker and Warburg, Andre Deutch, and Faber.[82]

Heinemann's African Writers Series emerged in the 1960s and published the work of Wole Soyinka (who had several of his plays produced at the Royal Court in London in the late 1950s), Chinua Achebe, and others. Longman Publishing launched an African and a Caribbean writers series, publishing novels and plays by Ken Saro-Wiwa, Jamaican playwright Trevor Rhone, and Trinidadian novelist Sam Selvon. Many of these Caribbean and African writers were also featured on the BBC's *Third Program* (until its cancellation in 1970), or in such BBC features as "Caribbean Voices." The lives of Caribbean migrants to the UK featured centrally in the work of many of the writers that appeared on these programs, such as that of Una Marson, George Lamming (novelist and critic from Barbados, and author of *The Emigrants*), and Colin MacInnes (Australian-English writer whose novels *Absolute Beginners, Mr. Love and Justice, City of Spades* all focused on Caribbean and African migrants to London). Selvon's novel *The Lonely Londoners* (1956), formed part of a trilogy (called the Moses Trilogy for its narrator and key protagonist) that chronicled the lives of Caribbean and African expatriates in London with humor and vibrancy. In an article on Sam Selvon's London-set novels, Susheila Nasta notes that London served as a center for Selvon and other Caribbean writers to develop a broader cultural identity as West Indians.[83]

While many writers wrote poetry and novels in the 1950s and 1960s about migration to Britain and the communities of Caribbean immigrants formed there, very few of them wrote for the theater. The aforementioned companies were active prior to and during the war, but there were no companies dedicated to Black theater active in the early postwar period. There were, however, actor-playwrights such as Errol Hill and others working in isolated productions and working to create opportunities for themselves and their fellow artists to work, and theaters such as the Royal Court and Theatre Royal Stratford East were hiring Black actors for their productions and occasionally producing work by African and Caribbean playwrights (such as Errol John, Wole Soyinka and Barry Reckord at the Royal Court).[84] Sandhu claims that "contrary to cultural cliché, [the metropolis] does not always feel imperiled by, or hostile to, 'marginal' culture…[but that] individuals (such as Laurence Sterne) and institutions (such as the BBC) have traditionally been very keen to encourage marginal voices."[85] Nevertheless, Judy Stone writes that playwright Mustapha Matura "…arrived in London in 1960 having never seen a play about Trinidad, never seen a play by a West Indian, never seen a play with a black cast."[86] A more active independent theater scene would emerge within the next decade, but in the early 1960s, opportunities for new playwrights to get their work produced were limited to the above venues and a few university drama departments.

Several playwrights, including Matura and Alfred Fagon, cite the social and creative expansiveness of the 1960s as a critical impetus for and influence on their writing for the theater.[87] In the early 1970s, plays such as Matura's *As Time Goes By* (Traverse Theatre, Edinburgh, 1971) and Alfred Fagon's *11 Josephine House* (Almost Free Theatre, 1972) marked the beginning of a wave of drama that focused on the domestic lives of Caribbean immigrants. The playwright Michael Abbensetts, who came to Britain from Guyana in 1963, had his first play, *Sweet Talk*, produced at the Royal Court Theatre in 1973.

Much of this theatrical activity depended upon the collective efforts of existing and newly created theater companies. In 1969, Jamaican actor Frank Cousins founded the Dark and Light Theatre Company, which "[…] aimed to be 'the first professional Multi-Racial Theatre Company in Great Britain" and to "promote understanding between people of different races through the media of the performing arts." Dark and Light produced a wide range of plays, from Errol John's *Moon on a Rainbow Shawl* to Georg Büchner's *Woyzcek*, to

Athol Fugard's *Blood Knot*, before financial difficulties, Cousin's failing health and other setbacks combined to sink the company in 1975.[88] Actor Norman Beaton and two others renamed it the Black Theatre of Brixton and attempted to launch a festival and a more activist theatrical agenda, but this too met its demise in 1978. Chambers cites the rise of another Black theatrical venture with community activist aims as a possible rival and then successor to the Dark and Light: the Keskidee Centre, which was founded in 1970 by Guyanese architect Oscar Abrams.[89] Keskidee played multiple roles within the community. Based in Islington, it offered social and educational services to African and Caribbean immigrants and their children, as well as sponsoring many forms of cultural events, from concerts to readings to exhibits. Keskidee also suffered numerous financial setbacks, from losses of grants to the costs of touring (the company toured Maori towns in New Zealand and organized London performances for such companies as the RAPP and the Theatre of Contemporary Arabic Drama).[90] For most of the 1980s, Keskidee struggled financially, and ultimately closed in 1992.[91] Its closure marked the loss not only of a critical provider of cultural and social services to the community, but also a physical and symbolic center or home sought by a marginalized diasporic community in London.

A third Black theater company looked poised to overcome the kinds of setbacks and difficulties that doomed the two previously described: the London-based Temba Theatre Company. Chambers frames the founding of Temba, by actors Oscar James and Alton Kumalo, as another effort at overcoming the marginalization faced by Black artists, who were often rejected on "the self-fulfilling grounds of inexperience."[92] Not only did Temba offer opportunities to actors, but also to playwrights, with an emphasis on producing new work for the theater. Under Kumalo's and then Alby James's leadership, Temba produced a wide range of plays, from musicals like Felix Cross's *Glory* to Trish Cooke's *Back Street Mammy* to adaptations of *Romeo and Juliet* (as an interracial romance) and of Thomas Mann's own adaptation of an Indian myth, *The Transposed Heads*. The Mann adaptation, *A Killing Passion*, turned out to be Temba's final production in 1992, when the company lost its Arts Council funding. Not only did the Arts Council's stated reasons suggest a pitting of all Black theater companies against each other (it noted its grants to the Black Mime Theatre and Talawa Theatre Company as indicators of its support for Black theater), but they also suggested a limited and essentialist vision of what audiences and material constituted fair game for Black theater companies.[93] In spite of the difficult conditions and restrictions for these companies, the 1970s and 1980s proved a prolific and active period for Black theater in Britain.

Additional companies such as Double Edge, the Theatre of Black Women, The Black Theatre Co-Operative, the Black Mime Theatre, and Talawa Theatre Company were all founded in this period.

Talawa was founded in 1986, nearly a decade after Tara Arts, but its founders had a similar desire to establish greater visibility and more multi-dimensional roles for Black British actors. Co-founders Yvonne Brewster, Mona Hammond, Carmen Munroe, and Inigo Espejel had extensive and wide-ranging experience in theater before joining forces to create Talawa. The quartet devised a name and a mission for the company that suggests both a political and a cultural agenda. "Talawa," a Jamaican idiomatic expression, connotes a quality that combines toughness with feistiness. The company profile cautions its reader that the name "...goes beyond the physical to mean dangerous," carrying the warning "[d]on't underestimate me."[94]

The company's mission statement suggests a firm conviction that theater can intervene in public discourse, both as a reflection of and an influence upon society. Its goals are stated as bullet points and reveal a vision of Black culture as both distinct from and integral to both national and transnational culture:

—to use black culture and experience to further enrich British theatre;
—to provide high quality productions that reflect the significant creative role that black theatre plays within the national and international arena; and
—to enlarge theatre audiences from the black community.[95]

Talawa's first production was a revival of Trinidadian author C.L.R. James's (himself a migrant to Britain in the 1930s) *Toussaint L'Ouverture*, a play performed only twice, in 1936, with Paul Robeson in the title role. James's parallel account of the Haitian revolution, *The Black Jacobins*, which was published two years later, in 1938, was a seminal work of revisionist historiography that continues to resonate with scholars of literature and history. James's depiction of the roles played by slaves, rebel leaders and free blacks in the fight to abolish slavery and establish independence in Haiti and of the constitutive impact of this movement upon the revolutionary struggle within France itself, reflects Talawa's dual commitment to exploring and illuminating black and European cultural resources and interrelated histories. Such commitment has been sustained through a repertoire that includes premieres of modern classics by African-American, African and Caribbean playwrights, new works by Black British playwrights, and revivals of European classics ranging from John Ford's *Tis Pity She's a Whore* to Oscar Wilde's *The Importance of Being Earnest*. Both Temba's and Talawa's work and mission parallel that of Tara Arts in their efforts to produce work that reflects the dynamism of their transnational and their local relationships.

British Asian theater artists also struggled to make a home for their work within the British theater world of the 1960s and 1970s. Some critics and scholars have commented on the challenges facing these artists. In 1976 Naseem Khan published a report for the Arts Council and the Community Relations Commission of Britain on the funding and development of "ethnic minority arts" throughout England, *The Arts Britain Ignores: The Arts of Ethnic Minorities in Britain*, which was the first report to document the work of South Asian language theater in Britain. The report's title and assessments strongly imply that the absence or neglect of work by Asian theater artists is a result of the constraint or the willful neglect of Asian arts by cultural institutions such as the national and regional arts councils.[96] In an overview of Arts Council policies regarding ethnic minority arts as they impact Black British theater, Barnaby King examines the mandate given Khan in the production of this report and the language and assumptions of subsequent documents that evaluate and express Arts Council Policy. He characterizes such language as indicative of the point of view of the paper as "written from the centre, looking out at diverse cultures all around and trying to create patterns out of them…Effectively, the Black Arts world is denied the ability to grapple for itself with issues of tradition and contemporary culture—this being seen as something which is the responsibility of the arts authorities."[97] A 1990 report written by Dr. B. Elizabeth-Clarke for the Arts Council, *Black Theatre in England*, examined the funding opportunities and needs for South Asian language theater and arts organizations. In their discussion of these reports, Graham Ley and Sarah Dadswell observe that although "theatre performed in South Asian languages has a rich and long-standing history in the UK…[and] both reports highlighted the valuable artistic contributions of South Asians to British society and the lack of funding opportunities available to them, neither functioned as a catalyst for funding opportunities for South Asian language theatre."[98]

What emerged instead at this time was English-language South Asian theater, and Tara Arts was the first company to perform in English. As Ley and Dadswell recount, "Not wishing to be associated with any one specific South Asian community or South Asian language, Tara chose to perform in English, thereby addressing the wider British public."[99] Jatinder Verma argues that it was the generation of Asians that emigrated from Africa and their children that produced most of the English-language live theater.[100] This generation would include Verma, who emigrated from Tanzania; journalist and playwright Yasmin

Alibhai-Brown, who emigrated from Uganda in the mid-1970s; and several others. Much of their work draws upon their double-diasporic cultural identity, incorporating not only Asian theatrical and linguistic elements, but also those acquired through their multigenerational presence in Africa, and fusing these with the British texts and practices of their current home. During the 1980s, more British-Asian theater organizations were founded. Among these were Hardial Rai and Poulumi Desai's Hounslow Arts Cooperative in 1980 (a multi-arts organization that combined arts and activism); Madhav Sharma's Actors Unlimited in 1981; Farrukh Dhondy's Asian Cooperative Theatre in 1983 (paralleling its contemporary Black Theatre Co-Operative in its emphasis on developing new writing for theater); Dominic Rai's Man Mela in 1989; Sudha Bhuchar and Kristine Landon-Smith's Tamasha Theatre Company in 1989; Rita Wolf and Rukhsana Ahmad's Kali Theatre Company in 1991; and Hardial Rai's directorship of Watermans Arts Centre (also in Hounslow) in 1992. These organizations produced theater and performance of widely varying forms, from documentary theater to sketch comedy to musicals to performance art, suggesting a diversity of Asian diasporic arts within the vicinity of London, let alone throughout the rest of Britain.[101]

Many of these companies and artists worked in the fringe venues and experimental stages around London, but by the 1990s, British Asian plays were beginning to find their way onto the national and regional stages. In 1990, the National Theatre invited Tara Arts to perform their "tradaptation" of *Tartuffe* as part of their repertory season that year. Playwrights Hanif Kureishi (whose first play, *Borderline*, was produced at the Royal Court Theatre in 1981) and Tanika Gupta had plays produced there as well, with Tara returning to the National in 2009 with their adaptation of Kureishi's novel *The Black Album*. The Royal Court Theatre, Birmingham Repertory Theatre, the Traverse Theatre in Edinburgh, the Leicester Haymarket, and the Hampstead Theatre are among some of the West End and mainstream theater institutions that have produced British Asian work. Nevertheless, British Asian and Black British theater artists have continued to find barriers to their full participation in the larger theatrical institutions and cultural agenda, and with rare exceptions, South Asian theatre has not been widely performed in these institutions either.[102]

Irish and Irish diasporic theater in Britain has had a very different history from Caribbean and Asian diasporic theater. Theater companies and plays from Ireland have a long history of production in national and regional theaters, as well as in fringe venues and in tours throughout Britain, not to mention those Irish playwrights in Britain whose work has become part of a canon of British literature (e.g., Richard Sheridan, George Bernard Shaw, and Oscar Wilde). Far more rarely, however, has work by or about the Irish diaspora in Britain been produced in British theatres. In the 1970s, London-based writers such as Mary O'Malley and Ron Hutchinson were producing works reflecting the Irish presence within Britain (in the thematic and formal elements of their plays as well as in their audience draw). In an essay on Irish immigrant fiction, Eamonn Hughes explains the absence of a body of Irish-British literature and of a hyphenated identity through the fact of Ireland's geographical proximity to England and by the stronger sense amongst its emigrants of the possibility of return.[103] Hughes stresses that such cultural and geographical proximity does not mean cultural affinity, but rather maintains that there is a paradoxical vision of England as site of liberation (from sexual, economic, and social constraints faced in Ireland) and oppression (through economic exploitation, discrimination, surveillance, and physical violence).[104] Such conflicting associations complicate the process, and the desirability, of assimilation into English society and culture for Irish migrants to Britain. Further, the proximity of Ireland to England allows for more permeability between their "national cultures." Tom Murphy's 1961 play *A Whistle in the Dark*, however, presents a complicated picture of such intercultural hostilities and rejections, as well as of the readiness to repress (or alternately, to produce) perceived "cultural differences" in order to be socially accepted.

In spite of these differences, and as noted above, Irish theater artists have typically worked individually with mainstream theater institutions (RSC, National, Hampstead, Royal Court, other West End theatres) and have gotten their work produced more widely. Irish writing has long been absorbed, even appropriated more readily by the British literary and theatrical establishment, while Asian, Caribbean, and African actors and directors have encountered much greater difficulty getting their work produced and finding roles, thus feeling a stronger impetus to form their own companies and work collectively to develop new work and produce classics from the African, Asian, and Caribbean canons. The commercial and critical success of contemporary Irish playwrights such as Martin McDonagh, Conor McPherson, Marina Carr, and Sebastian Barry on British stages represents one aspiration of Verma's. When asked by journalist Yasmin Alibhai (now Yasmin Alibhai-Brown) in 1986 where Tara would find itself in ten years' time, Verma replied: "A truly national institution. For us and all black arts to have broken into places like the Royal Shakespeare Company and the National Theatre. The day the National Theatre produces an Indian classic, it will become my national theatre."[105]

Verma's aspirational vision of twenty-odd years ago seems partly realized in the present theatrical landscape. Numerous studies of the past ten years have asked: Is theater keeping pace with other institutions (or leading) in terms of responding constructively to the changing demographics and other social conditions in Britain? Are there greater opportunities for inclusiveness and diversity within theater, and do they reflect British national and local engagement with the world? Recent closures of highly regarded Black British theater companies as Temba and others, due to losses of funding, might indicate that some of the opportunities for independent Black British companies and artists which were capitalized upon in the seventies and eighties have disappeared. On the other hand, it could be argued that such opportunities are now more available within mainstream theater venues like the National Theatre, the RSC, or the Royal Court, whose production calendars and casting choices reflect both an interculturalism and an encouragement of new writing that may reflect this diversity to a limited extent.

These competing perceptions of immigration to Britain and its role in defining British culture resonate strongly with the ways that British theater history is recounted and its influential figures and forces traced, even in work focusing on the postwar or contemporary period. Recent surveys of British postwar theater such as former National Theatre director Richard Eyre's *Changing Stages* or Dominic Shellard's scholarly *British Theatre Since the War* offer well-detailed accounts of theatrical movements and productions linked to their cultural and political context, but they include little or no mention of the contributions of immigrant or minority playwrights and companies. Other recent projects, however, have contributed their voices to these narratives and have made production materials and information more readily available for future scholars. In literary and theater history alone, initiatives such as Middlesex University's Asian arts archive SALIDAA, Exeter University's British Asian Theatre Archive, the Irish Theatrical Diaspora Project, the Theatre Museum's research guides, and Susheila Nasta's work on South Asians in Britain, among still more such projects, are reframing the stories told about British national and local histories.[106]

Chapter Three

JOURNEYS AND ARRIVALS

Remembering is an act of imagination. Any account we make of our experience is an exercise in reinventing the self. Even when we think we're accurately reporting past events, persons, objects, places and their sequence, we're theatricalizing the self and its world.

—W. S. Di Piero, review of Luc Sante's *The Factory of Facts*, *New York Times Book Review*, March 8, 1998

For many immigrants, the process of reaching and living in Britain is fraught with profound social and emotional upheaval, economic deprivation, and even violence. Postwar Britain has offered its immigrants relative political stability and economic opportunities, but it has also subjected many to extreme social marginalization and cultural dislocation and failed to protect them from individual or institutional abuse and oppression. At their best, plays about immigration find imaginative and visually striking ways to knit the personal experiences and memories of migration with the collective impact of such experiences and the forces that conditions them. With some plays, the scenes of departure establish indelible frames through which the audience comes to understand the stakes of migration for the migrants and for those left behind. Other plays might present the journey to Britain as a performance of the very improvisational and translational skills demanded of migrants, as the audience shares in the characters' disorientation, confinement, reconfiguration of their space, and imaginative tactics of survival. For instance, some recent dramatic works have staged such journeys by setting part or all of their action within the vehicles used by the characters to reach Britain, as in Clare Bayley's *The Container*, which placed both the audience and characters within an actual, albeit stationary, container truck during the play's premiere at the Edinburgh Theatre Festival in 2007. The characters in *The Container* are migrants who have been smuggled into and across Europe, and the play's action is contained entirely within and around this truck. Tara Arts' 2002 *Journey to the West* trilogy features an early scene of a dhow sailing from India to Africa, with the actors creating the bow of the ship by stretching and weaving ropes and sticks across the stage while they perform the voyage scenes, and then rearranging these materials into the railway system the characters are building on their arrival in East Africa. Comedies and musicals such as *The Big Life* and *Passports to the Promised Land* depict the docking of ships from the Caribbean at Tilbury Docks, reenacting the arrival scenes of the "*Windrush* generation" from the postwar newsreels and newspaper photos. These scenes depict the migrant characters' experiences in the moment, prompting the audience members to encounter Britain with the characters.

Plays such as these might also show us how such dislocations disrupt and remake migrants' relationships to their past and to the communities they leave behind. They can also illuminate the ways migration can risk devastating loss while forcing (or prompting a more voluntary) self-reinvention and self-mythologization. As depicted in the moment and through their reminiscences or memories, these characters' journeys may also involve a metaphorical death and rebirth, as they depart for Britain and are remade by their encounters and experiences. The plays often depict such experiences as gaining new significance with time or age, whether by having their characters recall their experiences from the perspective of their older selves, or by portraying their newly arrived migrant characters' encounters with more seasoned or settled immigrants. At the communal level, the societies that these migrants leave can form their own identities and mythologies through their emigrants' departures and returns. Plays such as Tom Murphy's *Conversations on a Homecoming* and Winsome Pinnock's *A Hero's Welcome*, for instance, explore the tensions wrought by an emigrant's return within the affected communities in rural Ireland and small-town Jamaica, respectively.

The plays most closely examined here dramatize the internal and interpersonal conflicts that arise from the push factors driving migration, the expectations of Britain held by migrant characters, and the reception that they receive in the UK. Whether as staged in the moment or as recollected through private flashback or reminiscence in dialogue, the scenes of departure for and arrival in the UK in these plays suggest that reaching Britain constitutes a new stage rather than an endpoint in these characters' journeys.

"Gold in the Streets": Myths of "Mother England" and the Shock of Arrival

The idea of England and the United States offering abundant opportunities for economic gain is suggested by the phrase, "gold in the streets," which inspired the title of the Belfast-based playwright Marie Jones' 1986 dramatization of Irish immigration to England in the twentieth century. *Gold in the Streets* was initially commissioned in 1985 by Camden Borough Council (in North London) for performance in community centers around the UK, and then was revised and expanded for a full production in Belfast and an extensive tour of Ireland and the United States. The play stages the stories of three women who migrate from Northern Ireland to Britain at three different moments in the twentieth century: Agnes, the wife of a weaver whose journey begins in 1912; Mary, a widow who migrates just after World War II; and Sharon, the wife of a policeman, who journeys to England in 1985. The women have different motivations for leaving their homes, from economic and social stagnation to sectarian conflict and fears of spillover violence. Their individual stories are linked, however, through this shared vision of England and the United States as possessing a material comfort and wealth that contrasts with the economic deprivation of their communities.[1]

Many other phrases have become part of the lore of emigrant societies and of those countries to which their emigrants journey. Neutral terms like "across the water" or "been-to" contain surprisingly layered associations with social status, emotional currency, and identity. The term "Babylon," popularly used in the Caribbean and in the diaspora, suggests a negative association of Caribbean, U.S. and European capitals with oppression. Similarly, the expression "The Big Smoke" conjures for many the soot and pollution encountered in London and British industrial cities. The former terms capture a measure of the hopes and expectations of migrants to Britain, while the latter terms paint a less than idyllic picture. All of these terms highlight the contrast between the emigrant locales (impoverished, largely rural, unpolluted, and often sunnier) and the UK (industrial, urban, sooty, rainy, and densely populated).

Many of the plays about immigration use the journey to and arrival in Britain to stage the tensions between immigrants' expectations of Britain and its inhabitants and the realities that confront them, whether through scenes that directly enact these experiences or through stories and memories recounted by the characters. For those migrants with a colonial education, London represented the center of a world made both familiar and aspirational through British history, geography, and literature lessons, lessons that typically inculcated an idealized image of British society and values startlingly at odds with what these migrants encountered. Such tensions can be comic, but they are also often poignant if not dangerous and suggest a widespread ignorance or naiveté about the UK.[2]

This initial ignorance drives the downward spiral of a recent immigrant from Trinidad in Mustapha Matura's satirical monologue *Nice* (1973), which recounts his comical misprision of others' advice about what to expect of the British and how to survive as an immigrant in 1970s London. Premiering at the Almost Free Theatre in London, the piece is written in idiomatic Trinidadian language, as are nearly all of Matura's plays. There are commas, but no periods throughout, giving the monologue the feel of a stream-of-consciousness narrative recounted by a man who seems lucid but naive. The naiveté diminishes as the story moves chronologically from "Wen a come off de boat…" to "da is the last time a go ever be nice ter anybody"[3] This man is in his mid-30s and uneducated, and seems to have friends who have advised him about how to get along in England. The story he recounts suggests that he is initially open and friendly, if opportunistic with friends and women, and then becomes a much more suspicious, worldly, exploited, and ultimately jaded Londoner through a chain of experiences that lead from his generosity to a friend to that friend's betrayal of him with his wife, to his ending up in prison for beating up the friend. In both the tone and substance of his storytelling, we see the trusting and generous immigrant for whom London is an oyster (much like the narrator of Selvon's *Lonely Londoners*, which has an extended stream-of-consciousness narrative similar to this one).

This transformation from naïve newcomer to jaded old-timer is a trope at least as old as Selvon's Moses. Hamon Williams, the patriarch of Edgar White's family drama *The Nine Night* (1983), says "All of us were disappointed when we got here," to which his friend and fellow migrant Ferret concurs, "I remember back home we hear so much about Oxford and Cambridge, the playing fields of Eton."[4] The two friends go on to share with each other how each had tried to join an English institution he held dear—the police force for Hamon and the church for Ferret—only to be rejected on the basis of their race. Hamon acknowledges his naiveté about the institutional racism of the police force (which has persisted well beyond the time frame of this play, as indicated by the

1999 report of the McPherson Inquiry into the London Metropolitan police department): "To show you just what a fool I was, when I first come, you know I tried to get in the police force," to which Ferret exclaims, "You joke!"[5] Speaking with the acquired experience of over twenty years spent in Britain, Hamon concludes that the "Englishman is a spin bowler, all the way."[6] In his remark, Hamon compares how the "Englishman" contradicts Caribbean migrants' expectations of British "fair play" and twists his own legal and political system to a cricket tactic. Ironically, it is a tactic that Caribbean cricketers have used to legendary effect.

Through their experiences as longtime peripheral observers of these institutions, both men have gained an insight comparable to the sharply-drawn characters of Selvon's Moses trilogy, written earlier than *The Nine Night* but set in this same postwar period. As with Selvon's Moses and some of his companions, Hamon and Ferret's accumulated experience with the realities of British society has elevated them to an insider-outsider status, providing them with knowledge that they can sometimes turn to their advantage. Selvon deftly depicts the ways that ambitious but naïve migrants are caught in efforts to deceive others (or deceived themselves), and sage old survivors like Moses manage to sustain themselves. Yet even the most skillful and wisest among them never manages to sustain his or her social security, material success and happiness consistently or simultaneously, and the novels and plays suggest that for those who seek it, such a combination will always elude their grasp.

The expectations held by native British of these migrants are profoundly informed by colonial constructions of Irish, African, Caribbean, and Asian otherness. Much evidence of this is anecdotal, coming in the migrant stories gathered and published on oral history or exhibition companion sites like *Moving Here* or *From War to Windrush*.[7] Complaints of Irish propensity for violence or Asian cooking smells, and of both of these groups' tendencies to crowd large families into small quarters are prevalent in migrants' historical accounts and in the plays. Such characterizations of these migrants connect implicitly to colonial discourse concerning the behavior and hygiene of these cultural groups. Stories told within the plays and in oral histories recount African and Caribbean children being asked by schoolmates in England if they had tails or if they were cannibals, or Irish children being associated with alcoholism and criminality. Anne Devlin's *After Easter* centers on Greta, Belfast-born but resident in England for most of her life, who says of her former colleagues and students in the rural school in which she taught, "They used to call me the Irish Art Teacher. And the girls used to say in front of me—as if to offend me, as if I cared: 'Father So and So's a bog Irish priest.'[8] While a bog literally refers to a mossy wetland, for the English schoolgirls (and perhaps also for some Irish city-dwellers) the term connotes rural ignorance.

Caryl Phillips' *Where There Is Darkness* dramatizes another common experience for postwar migrants from the above places: racial discrimination by landlords or realtors. In a scene set in the late 1950s, recently arrived Caribbean migrants Muriel and Albert Williams are welcomed by another migrant who has lived in England for eighteen years. Their new guide, Vince, warns the couple that "In England is legal law to put up a sign saying 'No coloureds in this house' or simply, 'No monkeys'."[9] Not only do such signs represent the more explicit face of what James Procter identifies as common exclusionary practices by landlords and housing agents in postwar Britain, but the latter phrase is an explicit legacy of colonial "science," which placed African and Afro-Caribbean people in a past and sub-human evolutionary stage.[10] Wole Soyinka's 1962 poem "Telephone Conversation," alludes to the disguised discrimination that often resulted in the "wasted trip" made by dark-skinned or Irish migrants responding to advertisements for vacancies. Soyinka's knowing and ironic tone suggests he shares Greta's and Helen's understanding of both explicit and implicit racism:

> The price seemed reasonable, location/Indifferent. The landlady swore she lived/ Off premises. Nothing remained/But self-confession. 'Madam,' I warned, / 'I hate a wasted journey–I am African.'[11]

Soyinka goes on to wryly portray the prospective landlady's racial anxieties through her response ("How dark?") to his description of himself as dark skinned. Like Devlin and Phillips, Soyinka filters this conversation through the point of view of the migrant, marking a perspectival shift from the more prevalent representations of such encounters in British literature or other art forms.

In addition to the associations with savagery or primitiveness so often received by British colonial subjects (in their home countries and in the UK), migrants in Britain face other forms of vilification, such as criminalization or even demonization. When asked about her newly acquired American accent, Greta's sister Helen replies, "London isn't a good place to have an Irish accent in [...] an Irish accent gets me followed round the store by a plainclothes security man."[12] The women's mildly sarcastic framing of these remarks suggests a familiarity with bigotry, suspicion and hostility carried with them from Belfast to England. Their anger seems less prompted by disillusionment than by an enduring intimacy with daily discrimination.

Young male immigrants or minorities in Britain are particularly branded or vilified in this way, whether as drug-running, homicidal "Yardies," fanatical "home-grown terrorists," scheming con artists, or some combination of these. Plays such as *Blood* and Kwame Kwei-Armah dramatize the ways both innocents and actual criminals can be subject to the same suspicion and targeting, as well as pressure from within their families and communities. In the aftermath of the terrorist attacks of 9/11 and 7/7 and the rhetorical and physical backlash against Muslim, Arab, and Asian residents of the UK and the United States, several plays directly addressed this vilification by staging the profiling and the imprisonment of suspected terrorists. Gillian Slovo and Victoria Brittain's 2004 play *Guantanamo: Honor Bound to Defend Freedom* (which premiered at the Tricycle Theatre) took the actual figures and setting of the Guantanamo incarcerations as their subject, while Nirjay Mahindru's *The Hot Zone* (first produced by Conspirator's Kitchen at the Lyric Theatre Hammersmith in 2005), presents a fictionalized drama that stages the arrest, imprisonment and interrogation of several British Asian and Asian men suspected of planning and direct involvement in past and future terrorist attacks. These plays speak to the experiences of "visible minorities" and the tensions within and between generations that are taken up in greater detail in the following chapters of this book.

Cold in the Streets?

Another common "shock of arrival" trope that is shared by many Irish, Asian, and Caribbean migrants is the confrontation with the urban landscape and climate of postwar England. Rather than "gold in the streets," migrants instead found it cold in the streets. Enda Delaney describes how the arrival in grey, war-ravaged London contrasted with Irish and Caribbean migrants' memories of the rural landscapes and seascapes of their home countries. He explains how Britain was the most "heavily urbanized country in the Western world" and speculates that this urbanization may have contributed to "unfriendliness," or to an anonymity and pace in British cities that was so markedly different from the small agrarian communities in Ireland, Asia, and the Caribbean from which many immigrants to Britain came.[13] In these places, residents knew each other intimately, possibly even to the point of social claustrophobia. In England, the chronic complaint of the plays' characters as well as Delaney's subjects is of the coldness of the climate and the people.

This alignment of climate and temperament is explicit in Harwant Bains' *Blood* (1989), which depicts the migration of Balbir and Manmohan, two Sikh cousins raised as brothers, from a rural village in Punjab to their shared "home" in Britain, a rooming-house in Shepherd's Bush, London, and then their own lives in London and Edinburgh. The play opens on the chaotic violence accompanying Partition, with a young Balbir witnessing two men kill and rape his mother and then force his father to kill himself on their promise to release Balbir. The subsequent scenes interpellate the sheltered perspective of Manmohan, who views their family as loving and secure, with the cynical outlook of Balbir, who places no trust in the family or in the nation and sets a pattern of manipulating others to empower and enrich himself. Their reaction to arrival in London illustrates Delaney's observation, as Manmohan complains "It's so cold, Balbir," to which Balbir replies, "It is a cold country."[14] Yet coldness is nothing new for Balbir, who has already suffered brutal rupture and cruelty that renders him orphaned and dependent upon the grace and good favor of Manmohan's father. Balbir swiftly sheds such dependence, perhaps recognizing the ways any familial ties render him vulnerable. Balbir learns to be cold in India, but it serves him well in Britain, and his ruthlessness pays off materially for him. Balbir's characterization suggests an alternate stereotype attached to immigrants, one that closely conforms to their aforementioned criminalization.

The coldness of the British climate and people features even more frequently in plays about Caribbean migrants. For instance, Tony Fletcher, young Guyanese migrant of Michael Abbensetts' *Sweet Talk* (1973)makes a joke of the climate, telling his Trinidadian wife, Rita: "This is Shepherd's Bush, not Port o' Spain, Trinidad. That's not sunshine out there, woman...! Only the English would call a night like this Spring."[15] Mustapha Matura's *As Time Goes By* (1971) features a marvelously caustic and extremely homesick young wife from Trinidad, whose response to her husband Ram's empty threat to send her back home is to say "Send me na, send me na, I don't care. It only cold an' dark over here."[16] While her husband Ram has figured out how to profit from some Londoners' expectations of Indo-Trinidadian mystics, Batee's own prejudices against Afro-Caribbeans and her anticipation of British hostility to immigrants prevent her from leaving her kitchen, where she feels an ownership she does not find elsewhere in the apartment or beyond it. When she does venture into the living room of their flat, she tells their visitor: "I don't like it [England]. I dying ter go back home, it too cold, de people don't like me, dey tink we is dirt an' de treat we like dirt, dey lazy and dey say we is lazy, dey dirty and dey say we is dirty, dey bad an dey say we is bad, how yer could like a place like dat?"[17] The complaints of the coldness of climate and reception greeting these characters often serves as a marker of homesickness, with these migrants' longing for warmth in England being both physical and emotional. This yearning manifests itself in such ailments as rheumatism, pneumonia, and chilblains, not to mention depression, alcoholism, and loneliness.

The contrasting fates and responses to the British climate and culture of these characters suggest that material and social success comes to migrants only at the expense of their emotional and spiritual lives. Where Ram's manipulation of British and immigrant expectations of him is largely benevolent (if personally profitable), Balbir's rise in power and affluence is propelled by his ruthlessness and ability to capitalize on the endemic corruption within Britain and India. Both plays invite the audience to sympathize with these characters' counterparts (Batee and Manmohan, respectively), even as they make the consequences of their weaknesses and limitations painfully visible.

The characters' accounts of the journeys and arrivals often signal how much wisdom or sophistication they have acquired through their experiences, as well as the degree to which they have retained or altered their values and ethics. The plays often convey this in flashback scenes or through reminiscences between a pair of friends, relatives, or a couple who have made the journey together. In the latter case, each of these characters serves as a kind of mirror and compass for their companion: the former allows the character to see him or herself a certain way, and the latter shows the character where he or she has gone off course.

Their reminiscences can prove divisive when they trigger contested memories or repressed trauma, but they can also serve to build communal or familial solidarity. A scene late in Ayub Khan-Din's *Rafta, Rafta* illuminates both possibilities, when the Indian immigrant couples and parents of the newlyweds at the heart of the play recall their early years in England. Eeshwar Dutt is the confident and financially successful father of one of the core families of this comedy. After the wedding between his son and the other central family's daughter, Eeshwar allows his vulnerability to show for a moment as he describes his own arrival: "It was the first time in my life that I was made to feel different… It was so shocking. It's hard to explain now, but it was the look people gave you."[18] His remarks prompt knowing and sympathetic reactions from the other parents, and they begin to open up and grow closer to each other as they share the excitement and anxieties of their arrival in England, and the devastating impact of the racist hostility and the rejection that they faced with the naiveté of newcomers. Their reminiscences provoke tension and shame, however, when the loss of a friendship and the circumstances surrounding it are discussed. This happens later on in the *Rafta, Rafta* scene described above, when Eeshwar tries to explain himself, "It's as if... as if it wasn't just me they were looking at. It was my family, my life, my whole world they were dismissing... But Brijesh was there...he knew who I was."[19] Brijesh is the name of Eeshwar's dearest friend, whose love for Eeshwar caused him to disappear suddenly from their lives after a secret attraction between Brijesh and Eeshwar's wife Lopa surfaces. Eeshwar remains unaware of the reason for Brijesh's disappearance, and continues to feel the loss keenly in the present of the play. Eeshwar's remarks suggest that Brijesh recognized in Eeshwar a personal history and qualities of character than no one else was able to see, or that went unacknowledged in his displacement from India to England. He contrasts this with the dehumanizing treatment that he encountered on his arrival.

In Caryl Phillips' play *Strange Fruit*, a single mother of about the same age as Eeshwar recalls experiencing even more dehumanizing treatment after her migration twenty years earlier to Britain from the Caribbean. Having encountered racism that leads to her dismissal from her factory job, Vivien finds herself broke and on the edge of starvation. She falls asleep on her bus ride to a job interview, overshooting her stop. Unable to pay the extra fare, Vivien is kicked off the bus and finds herself in an unfamiliar neighborhood where the strangers from whom she seeks help instead heap abuse on her. In recounting the story to a longtime friend and fellow migrant, she contrasts the misery of her experience with the anticipation she had felt prior to coming to England. She notes the irony in the fact that this afternoon marked her first experience of snow, which brought her shame rather than the joy she'd expected to find. Her story, recounted in the midst of her anguished estrangement from her two grown sons, acquires an added pathos. She and her friend Vernice share both the past disillusionment with England and the present despair over their children. Despite working her way out of poverty and providing her children with a secure home, Vivien seems unable to gain their respect. Like Eeshwar and Brijesh, the two women recognize in each other a worth that others do not. Unlike Eeshwar, Vivien's friend remains in her life, and in the absence of their life partners and no hope of a welcome for them in their home villages in the Caribbean, the two women try to sustain each other. In spite of Vernice's support, however, Vivien loses her will to live.

Such moments also illustrate the ways that reminiscing can both reinforce and disturb these characters' self-image and their personal mythologies. Much of the conflict and tension in these plays centers on the ways that characters' versions of their past and present selves don't quite coalesce into the kind of "immigrant success story" they would like to embody. Such a story would involve a steady progression from the shock of arrival to the adaptation to the culture and climate of Britain, to the acquisition of material success and social status, and finally to the triumphant return (permanent or temporary) to the home country. The marginalization and isolation that they face in Britain often expresses itself through their relationships to homes and to communal belonging, whether the kind of "dwelling spaces" described by James Procter, or the anticipation of a warm welcome as a returned emigrant.

Homeward Bound: The Dream of Return

It is in this hope and vision of return that so many of these characters' self-image is invested. In Kwame Kwei-Armah's 2003 play *Elmina's Kitchen*, the central character's Caribbean-born father expresses just such a hope:

> Let's go home together na? Open a little something in town. Show them bitches that Clifton can bounce back. Clifton have something. He children amount to something. You know they does laugh at me home? […] Let we go home show them that my seed is something. We are somebody.[20]

Elmina's Kitchen and other plays suggest that these visions of return are strongly gendered, with male characters like Clifton often seeking the abovementioned triumphant return, and female characters often acting on a sense of longing or of familial duty. Greta, the Belfast-born migrant to England of Anne Devlin's *After Easter* (1994), leaves her husband and family in England in response to an emotional breakdown and spiritual crisis that prompts her to return to Belfast to resolve her confusion. Her return is an expressed effort to overcome a growing sense of alienation and voicelessness she has experienced in her life in England. Enid Mathews, the Jamaican immigrant and mother in *Leavetaking* feels tremendous anguish and guilt at cutting her ties with her family in Jamaica at the urging of her mother. Each of these characters struggles with the emotional cost of raising children in a country that devalues them, while also acknowledging their estrangement from the "homes" from which they emigrated. Many of these plays illuminate the ways that emigrants' relationships to their source communities and families shape not only the possibility of their return, but also their desired conditions for such return.

For the male characters in many of these plays, the vision of return follows a self-mythologizing script that has them arriving in their home villages with all the stature and visible trappings of the successful emigrant, to be greeted with fanfare and a warm welcome. The false bravado of the title characters of Jimmy Murphy's *Kings of the Kilburn High Road* (2000), and the ritual reenactments of the moments of departure and arrival for the migrants of Enda Walsh's *The Walworth Farce* (2007) and Sol B. Rivers' *48/98* (1998) are distinct yet parallel forms of these visions. Such a return never comes to pass in the plays; more often than not, these characters often become trapped in emotionally and economically deprived lives in Britain, where they sustain themselves through various forms of denial. The dissonance between expectation and outcome seen in these plays runs through popular songs such as The Pogues' "Fairy Tale of New York" and Christy Moore's "Missing You", the latter of which which tells the story of a homeless "chippie" (carpenter) who has left Ireland in 1986 to work in England and now lives rough in London's "nobody zone",where he'd "give all for the price of a flight" but will "never go home now because of the shame".[21] Lord Kitchener's calypso songs emphasize the buoyant expectations of post-war migrants from the Caribbean, and as Stuart Hall notes, also touch on the disillusionment that often came when a migrant 'reach' Britain and finds no jobs and a hostile "welcome".[22]

The tensions in these plays often erupt when such forms of denial are exposed, and a character's (or characters') true situation is confronted. Much like the singer in "Missing You," shame and pride drive the characters of Jimmy Murphy's *Kings of the Kilburn High Road*, as the title ironically intimates. Murphy's play focuses its action around the formerly frequent, now less regular gatherings of a group of middle-aged Irish immigrants to London. Kilburn is a neighborhood of northwest London with a history of Irish and Caribbean settlement, and is very close to Willesden, another area of London made famous as an immigrant neighborhood through Zadie Smith's bestselling novel *White Teeth* (2000) and more recent *NW* (2012). Kilburn is also the home of the Tricycle Theatre, a building-based theatre known for its productions of Irish, Caribbean, and South Asian drama and since the opening of its cinema in 1999, for screenings of Bollywood films as well. Murphy's play was first produced by Red Kettle Theatre Company in Waterford, Ireland in 2000, but fittingly had its London premiere at the Tricycle Theatre (located on the Kilburn High Road) in 2001. It has since been made into a film that was Ireland's nominee for the Academy Awards in 2008. In the play, the men bemoan an England and an Ireland that neither values nor even includes them in their newfound prosperity and national confidence. One of the men, Jap, says "This tiger bastard [a reference to the "emerald tiger", or Ireland's economic 'boom' of the 1990s], want to get a piece of it before it's made extinct," a line that carries particularly painful resonances given Ireland's past and current economic struggles. When the men discuss returning, the bravado they initially showed about making money and returning in triumph falters. Another one of Kilburn's kings, Maurteen, notes the widening gap between their hopes on arrival in London and their current outlook: "Nearly thirty years since we all cem over to make our fortune. Said we'd return with it in sackfulls. The only thing now we could fill a sack with is lost chances."[23]

Both Devlin and Murphy capture the complex and often conflicting visions of the "home" each of the characters has left behind. In critical and often explosive exchanges, the audience discovers how social and familial prejudice and privilege shape the characters' relationships to each other and to the communities on either end of their journeys. For instance, Maurteen's friend Shay regards his hard-luck life in London as relatively easy compared to the social claustrophobia he felt in Ireland: "Home me bollox. [...] That's right. I made me bed and it's better than any bed I left behind in fuckin' Ireland! A pigsty, that's what I left behind me, a fuckin' pigsty...all of us did."[24]

Much like Vivien in *Strange Fruit*, Mamma Decemba, in Nigel Moffat's play of same name (produced in 1985 by Temba Theatre Company), has achieved greater financial security than the "kings" of Kilburn. She lives on in the play's present with only the ghosts of her friend Mertel and her husband John, however, both of whom emigrated with her from Jamaica (while still living). Like Vivien and Vernice, Mertel and Mamma Decemba share a grief over the lives their children lead in the UK and their own estrangement from or lack of control over them. Their aim of establishing better lives for themselves and their children seems utterly hopeless in the present of the play. Instead, the play unfolds as a near monologue lamenting the "lost opportunities" and alienation in ways similar to the men in *King of the Kilburn High Road*. Like these men, Mamma D and her husband John had no intentions of remaining in Britain and like them as well, saw their hopes of return diminishing year by year with each milestone of their lives in Britain. Unlike these men, however, Mamma D dreams of success for her children and a peaceful death for herself, a wish perhaps tied more closely to her old age than of her gender.

From Foothold to Bolthole

Of the men in *Kings*, two characters start families in Britain, and the others remain ambivalent bachelors (in or out of long-term relationships), a pattern that closely matches the demographics of postwar Irish migration, with many

Irish emigrants arriving to the UK single and remaining so or marrying and settling throughout Britain.[25] Of the Irish, Asian, and Caribbean migrants who were married, most left their families behind and travelled alone to work in the UK, with more of the Asian and Caribbean migrants sending for their children or wives (most married migrants were male) and children to join them later. Plays such as *Blood*, *Where There is Darkness* and *Sweet Talk* dramatize the particular challenges in reuniting and holding families together.

In *Blood*, Manmohan sends for and remains married to his wife Surinder after her arrival in the UK, while in *Sweet Talk*, Tony and Rita Fletcher (Caribbean migrants who married and then migrated together) are forced to send their son to Tony's mother's parents in Trinidad when Rita falls ill. *Where There Is Darkness* depicts the breakdown of Albert Williams' first marriage and his wife's return to the Caribbean without her husband and son as driven immediately by Albert's infidelity and cruelty and her belief in her inability to raise a child alone in either country, and more remotely (but equally strongly) by the alienation and homesickness she felt in Britain. These plays suggest the insidious effects of both material deprivation and material success, as these characters' happiness and financial success seem determined less by work ethic and investment of effort than by luck or unscrupulousness. These effects are compounded by the ways that everyday racism erodes their trust in the host population and reinforces their determination to maintain a wall between their domestic and working lives. This determination is tested more profoundly as many of these migrants shift from an imagined or real temporary dwelling to more permanent settlement in Britain.

These plays' depictions of immigrant journeys and arrivals and of their early efforts to make themselves at home in Britain illuminate the ways in which many immigrants find their position within British society to be precarious and indeterminate, a sense certainly reinforced for many by the violence that claims immigrant and minority lives with apparent impunity, and the harassment that many suffer on a daily basis. With long-term or permanent settlement come the challenges of aging, of (for some) raising families and sustaining marriages in the face of these dangers and of changing cultural expectations and circumstances. The following chapters examine the ways such intragenerational and intergenerational challenges shape these immigrants' and their children's visions of "home" and of their personal and cultural identity.

Chapter Four

PATRIARCHY
IN CRISIS

In the decades following the war, the majority of immigrants to Britain from its former colonies and from Ireland, male and female, were single or travelling alone and leaving families behind. Some of the plays set during this period depict these initial journeys through the reminiscences of characters with partners and families in the plays' present, as suggested in the previous chapter, but most of these characters arrive in England alone or with one friend, and then typically either send for their families later or marry and start a family in Britain. Their experiences seem to match those depicted by playwrights such as Mustapha Matura and Tom Murphy, who arrived in the UK without families during this period from Trinidad and Ireland, respectively. This chapter shifts us from the bedsits and boarding houses that often served as first stops on the immigrants' arrival in the UK (and, for some, was both first and final dwelling place) to flats and houses that suggest a firmer foothold in their communities, or the "bolthole" to which many aspired. Nevertheless, the characters' place within these communities and these domestic spaces reveal themselves to be precarious and fraught in their own ways.

Many plays that treat the lives of immigrant families in the UK dramatize the tension felt in adapting to the demands of their new environment and in negotiating different (and often conflicting) cultures. By setting these plays within the households inhabited by these characters, the plays enact the cultural collisions and fusions as they are most intimately lived and internalized. Plays that depict immigrant familial life tend to adopt the conventions of social realism and to feature patriarchal figures who, if not central to the action of the play or within British society, wield the most power within their homes and families. These disparities in position and power and their impact upon the lives of these men and their wives and children constitute the core conflicts and tensions in the play. The plays suggest that their disempowerment in society stokes an insecurity and volatility in these men as they struggle to assert their power within the home.

In their staging of the experiences of immigrant families in England, these plays present complicated versions of such displacement and marginalization. Places and characters located offstage make their presence felt in the interactions of the characters onstage and in their relationships to their living spaces. The plays treated in this chapter feature patriarchs whose efforts to control the fates of their families have widely varying consequences. The plays depict these families as interdependent, almost symbiotic organisms, even as the intermittently present patriarchs and the values they uphold shape the lives of its members. Comparable plays such as Edgar White's *The Nine Night* and Caryl Phillips's *Where There Is Darkness* present a different power dynamic. Their plays present Caribbean-born patriarchs who have achieved material success and a degree of prestige within their communities in England, yet suffer a profound disillusionment with their lives as their children begin to challenge their views and their position within their families. These characters recount their struggles with racism and the ways it has informed their working and social lives, while also revealing, not always unconsciously, the ways in which their male privilege has allowed them freedoms and opportunities not accessible to their female contemporaries. These patriarchs often vocally affirm their rights to such privileges in the end. At the same time, however, the plays introduce currents of dissatisfaction and resistance through these men's memories and insecurities and through the perspectives of some of the other characters, which leaves each patriarch with a profoundly shaken sense of entitlement and identity.

One of the earliest of these plays, Tom Murphy's *A Whistle in the Dark*, sets its tragic action in the late 1950s, in the wake of peak Irish emigration and amidst postwar deprivation and social repression both there and in Britain. The play dramatizes the volatile and tense relations within a family of Irishmen in Coventry, their repercussions for the eldest brother's marriage to an Englishwoman, and the ultimately tragic consequences for the whole family. Violence features equally poignantly and ominously in a more recent tragicomedy that, like *Whistle*, captures the volatility of a patriarch who is marginalized within his 'native' and 'host' cultures, as well as his diasporic community. British actor and playwright Ayub Khan-Din's first play, *East Is East* (1997), is set in the early 1970s, also a period of economic deprivation in England (particularly in Lancashire, where the play is set) and of large-scale immigration, at this time mainly by Asian migrants from East Africa. *East Is East*'s young protagonists are the children of a father born in Pakistan and a mother born in Salford (an area of greater Manchester).

Program cover for Tamasha Theatre Company and Birmingham
Repertory Theatre production of *East is East* (1996).
(Photo provided by Tamasha Theatre Company.)

The domestic spaces we see in these plays act as threshold spaces that bridge the worlds of London, Coventry, Salford, Mayo, Pakistan, Jamaica, and to some extent, even Bradford. The audience only sees these "original" places through the characters and settings of the plays; in other words, they imagine the contested versions of the characters' "ideal" homes versus the inhabited rooms shown to the audience. Institutional racism and violence against immigrants (or racially motivated violence) in English society are remotely depicted in these two plays, while other forms of social upheaval and cultural disorientation act more visibly and immediately upon the interior lives and the interactions of the characters. Their settings reflect a British culture very sharply divided into either-or categories. Characters shuttle between nostalgia and pragmatism, between "traditions" attributed to their countries of origin and the pressures of assimilation to an equally mythical British culture. These plays highlight the perceived cultural differences between a Britain still associated with a largely white Anglo-Saxon "heritage" and immigrant and minority individuals (and communities) still marked as racially or ethnically "other" to that Britain, in which there is dubious potential for assimilation, and even less for integration.

Homi Bhabha best captures the implications that wide-scale cultural dislocation, particularly postcolonial dislocation, has for the "house of fiction," and by extension, its counterpart on the stage. He argues that the "deep stirring of the unhomely" echoes within this space, a stirring that unsettles the boundaries suggested by its walled enclosures. Bhabha continues:

> In a feverish stillness, the intimate recesses of the domestic space become sites for history's most intricate invasions. In that displacement, the border between home and world becomes confused; and, uncannily, the private and the public become part of each other, forcing upon us a vision that is as divided as it is disorienting.[1]

Bhabha's analysis is trained on the "house of fiction" and on a process of reading that is intensely private, while these plays are quite differently aimed at public presentation. Yet his analysis of this particularly postcolonial uncanny, and of its dissolution of any sense of security or sanctuary in the domestic realms of these novels, resonates strongly with these plays. For the migrants in these plays, this uncertainty meshes with an equally profound sense of familiarity with many aspects of British culture and history, among them the stereotypical and embedded perceptions held of them by those they encounter in England.

The erosion of divisions between these spheres of life within the plays' settings gains an additional permeability through realist theater's "fourth wall," which connects the audience with the sliced-open living spaces of the plays. For these characters, their living spaces can be as dangerous to them as public places, if not more so for containing more profoundly and intimately lived conflicts. These plays enact the imaginary constructions of home, of self, and of community, which enable both the accommodation to and the transformation of the conditions of cultural displacement.

The plays' depictions of intimate and familial dwelling spaces as realms of violence, marginalization and tension parallel the images of diasporic conditions and dwelling spaces presented in much of the work of Palestine-born visual artist Mona Hatoum. Her video art and her installations speak to experiences of exile extending beyond (but often referring to) her own double dislocation from Palestine in 1948 and from Beirut in 1975 (the latter by the Lebanese civil war). "Homebound," Hatoum's 2000 installation at the Tate Britain, presents a domestic environment that meshes the familiar with the hazardous, visually echoing the tensions sustained in the plays. Kitchen furniture and appliances are arranged in a room and laced through with wires that sputter with live currents, and a crib frame is stripped of its cushioning to expose knife-sharp slats. The idea of home as a refuge or as a site of comfort is here undermined by the hints of prisons and internment camps that haunt this domestic scene. The installation suggests how spaces associated with nurture and security can be unstable sites of traumatic injury and alienation. Many domestic dramas enact similarly paradoxical situations, with the intimate domesticity of the rooms containing the violent and conflicting feelings within and between the characters. In the play *East Is East*, George's love for his English wife Ella is a source of insecurity and even shame for him, as it undermines his insistence that his children submit to arranged marriages. The sense that their parents' marriage enacts what their father warns them against makes George and Ella's children question their own identities, making them insecure or resentful. Home is where they come to find comfort and a sense of belonging, and to take refuge from the hostility they may face in the outside world, but their sense of self-esteem is constantly undermined, their personal autonomy continually denied them, which leads them to view their home as a site of imprisonment. Irish playwright Enda Walsh's *The Walworth Farce* comically but poignantly enacts the mental imprisonment of exile and the ways in which the home (in this case a flat on the Walworth Road in South London) becomes both a refuge from a hostile outside world and a site for an endless rehearsal of departure and violent rupture. Dinny, the patriarch of Walsh's play, exerts his authority in a literally theatrical way, both scripting and directing his sons in a ritually repeated performance of their last day in Ireland. *The Walworth Farce* had its premiere at the Edinburgh Theatre Festival in 2007 and since then has toured throughout the UK, Ireland, and the United States.

Hatoum's installation demonstrates the precariousness of domestic life in the face of exile, dispossession, war, and severe economic deprivation. The installation visually and aurally normalizes the situations that render home a utopian dream for diasporic individuals and communities. The title of Hatoum's exhibition, "The Entire World as a Foreign Land," evokes an alternative vision of the "normal" or the "familiar," one in which the exilic perspective and the provisional existence are the commonplace conditions. As Edward Said writes in his introduction to the exhibition catalogue:

> An abiding locale is no longer possible in the world of Mona Hatoum's art, which, like the strangely awry rooms she introduces us into, articulates so fundamental a dislocation as to assault not only one's memory of what once was, but how logical and possible, how close and yet so distant from the original abode, this new elaboration of familiar space and objects really is. Familiarity and strangeness are locked together in the oddest way, adjacent and irreconcilable at the same time.[2]

For migrants driven by economic and political factors, the familiarity and comfort of domestic spaces are also often laced with the conflicts, tensions, and hazards of life between homelands. Said's description aptly characterizes the worlds presented in *A Whistle in the Dark* and *East Is East,* in which the suspension between familiarity and strangeness is perpetually and often menacingly charged. Intimate and domestic spaces (and relations) are particularly vulnerable to both explicit and subtle incursions and eruptions of violence. Just as the live wire crackles through the rooms of "Homebound," constantly live currents of tension electrify the plays' settings and their characters' interactions. In *Whistle in the Dark*, the result is an unease throughout that resembles that of Harold Pinter's plays, particularly *The Homecoming* (1965), which has prompted speculation that Murphy's play influenced Pinter. In *East Is East,* such tension carries a greater poignancy, even as it is frequently broken by hilariously comic moments.

These plays also parallel Hatoum's work by using domestic space to explore the links between local and international affiliations as well as between personal and national identities. They fuse the themes of her art with a realist approach that exposes several crises in postwar British society. As much as they reflect the challenges of intercultural conflict and displacement, the plays also powerfully depict the cultural dislocations at work within these societies. While they are written and set in different periods, their dramatization of the diminishing status of the patriarchs at the center of these plays highlights how not only immigration and emigration, but also other forces at work within these societies are reshaping the roles and expectations of men and women, with both positive and negative implications. Both plays portray characters who struggle with others' expectations of them, often based on cultural stereotypes, gender roles, and familial as well as communal codes.

Cultural stereotyping has continued to be a volatile issue in British theater, although with perhaps a less imperative "burden of representation" for Irish drama. British Asian and Black British drama has yet to experience the kind of proliferation and integration into the West End and national stages that Irish drama has, and Asian and Caribbean drama is far less frequently produced in such venues. *East Is East*, a co-production by London-based Tamasha Theatre Company and Birmingham Repertory Theatre opened in London in 1997 at the Royal Court Theatre, and then transferred to the Theatre Royal Stratford East. By this time, London theaters had housed countless urban working-class dramas, thus its location (in Khan-Din's actual hometown of Salford, Manchester) invited far less attention for its socioeconomic setting than for its farcical comedy and for the compelling interplay of cultural, class, and personal loyalties it presented. The production marks the most celebrated of a host of highly acclaimed theater and television productions of the 1990s dramatizing the lives of Asian-British families, among them the sketch comedy *Goodness Gracious Me*, the stand-up comedy of the Funjabis, and several other productions by Tamasha Theatre Company. The play proved to be a box-office success for both the Royal Court and for the Theatre Royal Stratford East. It was subsequently adapted into a hugely popular and award-winning 1998 movie. While the character of George Khan embodies a number of stereotypes, the multidimensionality of his characterization and the timing of the play's production may have mitigated any accusations of caricature or stereotyping. In fact, its critical and public reception shows that Khan-Din's depiction of a violent Muslim patriarch did not necessarily produce the politically charged or polarized public responses it might have either a decade earlier or in more recent years.

Tom Murphy's *A Whistle in the Dark* was the first to focus on postwar immigration to England, and was produced in 1961 by the Theatre Royal Stratford East. This theater was also the site of the 1956 London premiere of Brendan Behan's play *The Hostage*, and of the 1958 world premiere of his play *The Quare Fellow*. Murphy's play takes place in late-1950s Coventry, a city that was heavily reliant upon Irish labor for its postwar reconstruction and industrial growth. *A Whistle in the Dark's* naturalism is cited by Nicholas Grene as a decisive factor in its success in Britain at this time, appearing as the realist plays of the "New Wave" were becoming commercial hits for the Royal Court.[3] The play, rejected by the Abbey Theatre in Dublin for its corrosive and decidedly "anti-pastoral" vision of Ireland and Irishmen, generated much controversy within London as well.[4] However, the play proved successful enough to merit a West End transfer, and its 1989 revival by the Druid Theatre Company was a critically acclaimed success for the Royal Court Theatre.

These plays' geographical and socioeconomic settings and formal realism place them within a "canon" of British theater and film which extends from the British New Wave into present-day social realism, one that links the plays of Shelagh Delaney and Arnold Wesker, and the films of Tony Richardson with later works that focus on working-class lives in multicultural contexts, such as Stephen Frears' not-quite-realist *My Beautiful Laundrette* (1985) or Ken Loach's *Ladybird, Ladybird* (1994) and *Ae Fond Kiss* (2004). As early as the 1950s, plays such as Shelagh Delaney's *A Taste of Honey* (Theatre Royal Stratford East, 1956) and John Osborne's *Look Back in Anger* (Royal Court Theatre, 1956) shifted the spotlight of realist theater to non-traditional families and working-class protagonists, marking a distinct change from the "country house" and middle-class centered plays of Terrence Rattigan, Noel Coward, and other frequently produced playwrights of the period. In his study of postwar British realist theater, Stephen Lacey argues that these plays represented a determined effort to redefine the subjects and space deemed worthy of dramatization:

> The realism of a set like this asks to be judged not only in relation to an observable social reality beyond the stage but also against other kinds of theatre; in both these senses, the play was a considered provocation. The set was an act of semiotic vandalism, challenging almost point by point the iconography of the bourgeois living-room and the country-house drawing-room…."[5]

Lacey cites the emergence of this theater as reflective of larger fissures within the consensus politics and culture of postwar Britain. Choosing two years, 1953 and 1956, to mark this societal shift, Lacey argues that the earlier year, symbolically linked to a New Elizabethan age by her Coronation, was a triumphalist time, in which England was (at least outwardly) more secure. Events in 1956 such as the Suez Crisis and the Soviet invasion of Hungary signaled the breakdown of consensus. Lacey writes: "The moment of 1953 offered images of coherence and stability, of a nation emerging from the vicissitudes of postwar recovery and pre-war class struggle with its traditions intact. The moment of 1956, however, offered images of dissent, instability, fracture and powerlessness."[6] London theatergoers were soon exposed to the direct and indirect responses of a younger generation of playwrights to such fissures. Coupled with their focus on class conflict and late imperial angst was a concern with the exclusionary politics of British nationalism.

In an ironic reversal of the prevalent imagery of the domestic space of "Little England" threatened by alien outsiders, both *A Whistle in the Dark* and *East Is East* stage differently constructed visions of domestic order and conflict. By confining the action of the plays within immigrant homes, these realist plays render visible the internal dynamics and tensions of the families and individuals within them. The plays stage the characters' struggles for belonging and their claims to communal affiliation in the face of impossible demands on or conditions for the fulfillment of those claims. The homes in these productions frequently emerge as spaces in which characters negotiate differently held values or expectations within themselves, their families, and their communities. Such negotiations manifest themselves in the everyday and in the exceptional practices of these characters. Through these practices, they illuminate the repercussions of cultural displacement and the processes of "making oneself at home" in an all-too-frequently hostile environment.

A Whistle in the Dark opens with the impending arrival of Hugh "Dada" Carney and Des Carney, the father and youngest brother of Michael Carney, their host and eldest son/brother. Visiting from their hometown of Grange in County Mayo (western Ireland), Dada and Des represent the inescapable past and the potentially bright future for Michael. Michael, in his mid-thirties now, has lived in Coventry for fifteen years, where he has married an English woman. For an unspecified amount of time, he has housed his three younger brothers, who have "made a name for themselves" in Coventry (and prior to that in Mayo, it emerges), through graft, violence, and petty crime. Dada and the brothers have a different future in mind for young Des, and resent Michael's appeals for Des to return to school and seek a professional career as high-handed interference. The play casts their clashing perceptions of Mayo and England as a battle of cultural and personal delusions and long-harbored grudges. Their cultural dislocation is not simply aligned with the conflictual relationship between Irish and English culture or with their geographical displacement, but also with the changes within both nations and their relationships to the world beyond their borders in the postwar (and post-independence) decade of the 1950s.

By the 1950s in Ireland, the civil war and subsequent violence had depleted an already strapped economy. Conditions in the west of Ireland (where Tom Murphy grew up) were bleak, and a devastating border war was being fought between the IRA and loyalist militias from 1956 to 1962. Throughout much of

Ireland, but especially in the west, the church controlled most aspects of rural and town life. Fintan O'Toole describes the educational and social institutions as very stratified: "The Christian Brothers saw themselves preparing boys from less well off homes for accession to the pinnacles of civil service jobs and company clerkships, the only social mobility available to the working class in a stagnant society."[7] Such outlets were only available to the boys who were favored or simply succeeded in school, an unlikely possibility for the Carney brothers. We see similar classism and social (and sexual) repression in the 1950s London Catholic school that features in Mary O'Malley's *Once a Catholic* (treated in the next chapter).

Like the fictional Carneys, peak numbers of Irish men (and as many women) opted to emigrate and find work in the industrial cities of England. Murphy himself was a migrant to England under slightly different conditions, leaving Ireland in his twenties in 1961 to pursue his playwriting career in London. For many Irish people, migration meant the separation of families, and work environments were often exclusively male (building sites and factories) and female (hospitals, domestic service, and social work). O'Toole reads many of these changes as they translate to the physical environment of the Carney household and the ways that the characters relate to it. He makes a strong case for viewing the brothers' occupation of the living room (as their sleeping quarters) and their treatment of Betty as indicating a resistance to their new environment: "We are taken immediately into a world where the normal physical arrangements of space which signify domestic order and civilization in modern urban society are being overturned [by the Carney brothers]."[8] Their total absence of respect for privacy or property also suggests a rejection of values they associate with Michael and with England, both direct targets of their scorn. O'Toole argues that they may derive their sense of space from rural housing in Ireland, in which extended families often lived in closer quarters that often fused living and cooking spaces with sleeping areas.[9]

The opening of the play thus presents the audience with a stereotypical "clash of civilizations" marked by the wild, unmannered Irishmen and the order-driven, polite Englishwoman. In the alignment of England with femininity in the form of Betty, the play ironically reverses a common trope of aligning colonized peoples and territories (here aligned with the domestic space) with the female body and its violation. In some ways, their occupation of Michael and Betty's home enacts the kind of "invasion" feared by the anti-immigrant movements mentioned in Chapter Two. Michael's brothers constantly taunt Betty, directing both passes and threats at her and referring to her as "English Polly." Their misogyny is quite easily readable: denigrating Betty as worthless "English charver," they hold her up against the ideal Irish woman (invisible, compliant, and economically productive—like their mother) and against the prostitutes for whom Harry pimps. They justify their abuse of the "interfering" Betty through their own brand of cultural nationalism, one that glorifies their family as not like the English even as they acknowledge its exclusion from Irish society. Their vision of Betty as potentially emasculating them by culturally domesticating their "Irishness" without being domesticated (i.e., submissive and silent), suggests their own sense of insecurity and potential for self-delusion. Their behavior seems to be a reaction to as much as a provocation of the discrimination that they encounter (both in Ireland and in Coventry), and Murphy's treatment of this symbiosis perfectly balances their viciousness with their own reservoirs of pain and disillusionment.

Towards the end of the fifties, Ireland was undergoing what Richard Kearney calls a "crisis of culture," precipitated by its moves towards becoming increasingly industrial, secular, and tied into the European Community. This crisis produced a sense of fragmentation and discontinuity, of a clash between tradition (or invented tradition) and modernity, and a conflict between a dying world and a world about to be born. He acknowledges that Ireland parallels postwar Britain in this respect, in this sense of a "breakdown of inherited ideologies and beliefs," yet he distinguishes Ireland as experiencing this crisis in a more profoundly shocking manner because of greater homogeneity of society/culture.[10] Fintan O'Toole argues that these changes posed a threat to the cultural nationalism underpinning the social and cultural institutions in Ireland at this time. Like Kearney, he identifies the shift to industrialization and internationalization as the critical force behind such changes. The economic changes were accompanied by social and cultural changes, which O'Toole attributes to the policies set in motion by Ireland's Finance Secretary, T. K. Whitaker:

> ...Whitaker was sowing the seeds for the abandonment of nationalism as an economic, and gradually as a cultural force.... the strength of the nationalist movement was its inclusiveness, the way in which it managed to find a place within its political programme for everything from social justice to religious righteousness, from the words the Irish were to speak to the games they were to play, taking theatre and literature effortlessly into its warm embrace.[11]

It is this nationalism that Dada and his sons simultaneously champion and mock, and, paradoxically, from which they are rejected even as it purports to include all Irish within its fold. Their relationship to Irish nationalism reflects a desperate need to belong to the imagined community and a simultaneous denial of that need through a substitution of familial bonding for social acceptance. According to O'Toole, the play's familial conflict reflects the struggle between a cultural nationalism that privileges images of a homogenous, quaintly archaic, and rural Ireland (the "authentic" culture of leprechauns and fairies, of myth and legend, of talk and drink, and, crucially, of anti-colonial political and cultural resistance) and an industrial European culture that privileges a mobile economy, privacy and cosmopolitanism. [12] O'Toole sees Dada as embodying this passing world, and his violence as fuelled by the desperation of sustaining his world-view and self-image in the face of changing conditions and social dislocation:

> Dada's fantasy of being at one with the respectable middle-class of the town is played by his drinking at the golf club [a parallel to the exclusionary male worlds of the Carney households—in which women, like Betty and like the boys' mother, are the neglected caretakers] with the architects and the doctors. He embodies the dream of nationalist Ireland, the dream of a country in which the common name of Irishman would serve to diminish the differences of class and status… The image of architect, doctor and dosser discoursing through the night in fluent Gaelic and drinking heartily at the golf club is a risible and pathetic fantasy which is the product not just of Dada's delusions of grandeur, but of a whole nation's political delusions.[13]

Murphy extends this connection between personal and national delusion into the central tragic action of the play. Exile in Coventry enables such delusions to be sustained unchallenged by confrontation with actual Irish society, much as Dada can sustain his self-mythologization as fearsome fighter by avoiding any actual combat with anyone other than his sons.

The play instantly establishes that violence and fighting have long been an integral part of Carney family life and reputation for multiple generations. Their ability to fight and confrontational tendencies are a source of family pride for the brothers and their father (except for Michael, who is non-confrontational and evasive). Key scenes and exchanges in the play show that there are deeper and broader forms of violence at work in their lives and their histories. References to the boys' school and church lives, their treatment by authorities in the town, and even their father's past work as a police officer suggest that aggression and physical abuse are inseparable from their lives outside and within their home. Likewise, in England, their legal and illegal activities often involve extreme physical danger, and their confrontational attitude seems both source and product of the violence in their home and work life. Michael's response to similar conditions is to withdraw and adopt a non-confrontational approach, believing that by doing so, he can ultimately transcend the expectations held of him. He is partly motivated by cowardice and partly by a genuine desire to reconcile his family with the society in which they live. Again, Betty is both a catalyst for and target of his shaken self-image and his need to assert his authority and masculinity within their house.

Michael's next brother, Harry, keenly picks up on the flaws in Michael's vision, and on the ways in which their family is perceived and defines itself against those perceptions. Harry's observations are tactically expressed to draw out the self-contradicting hypocrisies of sycophantic friends like Mush, and of well-intended critics like Michael. Harry is contemptuous both of English racism and of the "Muslims," or Asians in Coventry. Nevertheless, he acknowledges the irony that even as they fight the Asian families, they are aware that their presence shields the Irish from the brunt of English racism. Further, the brothers acknowledge their respect for the Asians' emphasis on familial loyalty and honor.

Harry sees the stereotyping of Irish in the English imagination, how they "wrinkle up their noses" at them, while Michael is equivocal, arguing that Harry and Mush exaggerate. Harry replies: "Your big mistake is thinking they don't do it to you."[14] Harry's response to their prejudices is to dedicate himself to fulfilling them: "So we can't disappoint them if that's what they think."[15] Harry knows that his actions doom him to further marginalization, but he views being feared and scorned as better than being ignored and scorned. Conscious of the social expectations held of them both in Ireland and in England, the brothers (except Michael) take them on as badges of honor. The play reveals the tensions between their world views, between a defiant cultural nationalism and defense of familial "honor" versus a pragmatic and non-confrontational assimilationism, while capturing the strengths and failings of both approaches. It also exposes the ways in which such ideals as "honor," cultural pride and pragmatism are exploited by each of them to sustain their positive self-images.

The reception of the play, both in Ireland and in England, highlights the pitfalls and ironies of these competing nationalisms. O'Toole recounts the production history of *A Whistle in the Dark* as an illustration of the reactionary mores of the Irish theatrical establishment. Murphy's play, which was originally titled *The Iron Men*, competed in several amateur playwriting competitions and won first prize in one. The play was championed by actor/producer Godfrey Quigley, who wanted to produce it for the Dublin Theatre Festival of 1961. When this possibility fell through, Quigley went to London to work, and while there took the script to Joan Littlewood's Theatre Royal at Stratford East, which eventually accepted it for production.[16] Before they accepted it, Murphy sent the play to Ernest Blythe, the Managing Director of the Abbey Theatre. Blythe responded with a scathing letter rejecting it and criticizing its characters and its atmosphere, which he said lacked any credibility. O'Toole cites his rejection as indicative of a dominant cultural nationalism operating at the Abbey (and pervasive within Irish society) which demanded naturalistic representations of an idealized Irish peasantry and rural culture.[17] Richard Kearney confirms this interpretation:

> Murphy may be said to belong to a counter-tradition in Irish drama to the extent that he poses a direct challenge to both the naturalism and folksy romanticism of the mainstream theatre of the Literary Revival. While this Revival was largely created in a metropolitan context for a metropolitan audience [both in Dublin and London] it promoted an idealized image of rural Ireland which corresponded to the emergent culture of Irish nationalism. In drama, the Revivalist movement was particularly associated with the work of the Abbey Theatre.[18]

With *A Whistle in the Dark*, the issue was less about form than content. The play provoked anger from Irish critics for what they perceived as unrealistically negative depictions of Irish men, or, where they accepted such depictions as accurate, for "portraying a side of Ireland best left unrevealed."[19] One critic of the post-London production at the Olympia Theatre in Dublin expressed dismay at the "picture of the Irish race that was paraded for three months last year to the wondering gaze of London theatregoers."[20]

Reactionary rejection of a dramatic challenge to conservative nationalism is not, however, the only way to read such responses. Amidst the ongoing discrimination against and abuse of many Irish nationals in Britain, there was genuine cause for concern about perpetuation of stereotypes of the Irish. The temptation to read these tensions as a conflict between Ireland's past and Ireland's future is a powerful one, one that draws on a deep reservoir of father-son clashes in Irish drama and literature.[21] Such an oppositional reading, however, also risks playing into the hands of audiences (and critics) all too eager to extend the stereotypes well beyond the world of the play, and to dismiss all Irish nationalist aspirations, and perhaps much of Irish culture, as regressive. Much of the critical reception was acutely sensitive to the subtler aspects of Murphy's theatrical exploration of such charged issues, and subjecting a theater review written under time pressure to the same scrutiny as a more sustained analysis of a playwright's body of work would be unjust. Nevertheless, certain telling responses to the play emerge in these reviews, and bear exploration.

In an often-quoted review of the 1961 production, noted *Observer* theater critic Kenneth Tynan calls the violence of the play, "...naked, immediate, and terrifying".[22] He continues, arguing that playwright Tom Murphy "...shoves the violence before our astounded eyes; and the result is arguably the most uninhibited display of brutality that the London theatre has ever witnessed."[23] This from a critic who has without a doubt sat through many a Shakespearean bloodbath: Is he truly astounded by several punches and an accidental fratricide that comes in the final scene of the play? Tynan's remarks do highlight a crucial aspect of *A Whistle in the Dark*, in that the play's violence is continually palpable, if not always made visible. The threat of violence is the current that electrifies the play, not as overt action, but rather as the fabric of a family life and a history that is conjured as much through talk, gesture, and intonation as through direct violent action. However, as Nicholas Grene suggests, the violence of the play and its characters are so closely aligned with the playwright and his nationality, that Murphy's artistic integrity gets overlooked in the critical response:

> On no personal knowledge, Kenneth Tynan, who claimed in his review that he would not like to meet Murphy in a "darkened theatre", here constructs Murphy as the wild Irish dramatist, out Behaning Behan. And the violence of his play...was seen as the loosing of raw, primitive Irish energies to shock and stimulate the overcultivated metropolitan audiences of London.[24]

The play is not wholly free from overt or "naked" brutality—but its allusive reliance on the props and threats of violence work a subtler and more terrifying magic on the audience's imagination and their perceptions of the drama unfolding onstage than Tynan here suggests. Moments such as Dada's unbuckling his belt and lashing the table with it, and Harry's knowing tap on Michael's shoulder with his iron horseshoe (his "souvenir from Ireland") carry much more powerful resonance for their implicit histories of abuse and repression than most onstage fights ever could. The pacifist-conciliator Michael, on the receiving end of both of these gestures, appears that much more reasonable, yet also more deeply passive, for these suggestions of past and future harm. The play's final scene suggests a critique of patriarchy in that Dada's pressure on his sons in the service of the "family name" and his own authority produces a fatal act of violence by his least violent son. This act separates the sons from the father and links them in their familial inheritance of violence.

Both *A Whistle in the Dark* and *East Is East* build the tension within their respective households through hints at and fears of repeating events that precede the play's opening. Patriarchs with guilty consciences drive the core conflicts of both plays. Each father's struggle against their increasingly superfluous role within his family and his marginalization within multiple communities inspires limited empathy (much more in George Khan's case). Nevertheless, their constant invocations of religious authority, cultural pride, and familial honor to force their will upon their families (usually at the service of deeply flawed judgment), exposes the hypocrisy and cowardice at the heart of their actions. Any fears that Khan-Din's characterization of George would be an invitation to "Paki-bash" were not borne out by the critical reception of either the play or the subsequent film, which read their treatment of George's cultural differences and religious beliefs as largely of his own making.[25] One cannot help but wonder if such a depiction would play differently in the highly-charged, post-7/7 (following the subway and bus bombings in London) cultural climate.

The critical reception shown *A Whistle in the Dark* suggests that latent cultural expectations and stereotypes often risk being reinforced by their onstage enactments. In his 1961 review, Tynan frames the play's weaknesses within his understanding of the broader context of Irish drama: "What blights the play is something endemic in the Irish temperament—a compulsion to turn drama into melodrama, and comedy into farce."[26] In the reception of the 1989 revival of *Whistle*, some critics confront the question of stereotyping more self-consciously, for instance, Charles Spencer of *The Daily Telegraph*:

> It is just as well that Murphy is Irish, for if an English man had written this play, he would be in deep trouble with the Race Relations Board. It burns with barely contained contempt for some of the playwright's fellow countrymen, reinforcing ancient prejudices about the "bloody Irish".[27]

His review discusses the pervasive stereotypes ascribed to the Irish that appear in the play, but it fails to acknowledge the characters' own awareness about and exploitation of these stereotypes and expectations. It is this awareness, explicitly presented in the conversations between Michael and his family, which enables the play to critique such stereotypes even as its characters might fulfill them. Harry's self-awareness is eerie, particularly in the way he uses it to both explain his viciousness and to unsettle Michael's complacency and self-righteousness. A few revealing conversations with Michael illustrate how Harry sees himself as emotionally scarred by childhood experiences of violent repression and by the casual but wounding insults directed at him at home and at school. He has an ironic detachment from himself and from his actions, however, that renders his actions colder and more menacing and that undermines any audience empathy with him.

Even in such apparently unredeemable characters, both Murphy and Khan-Din offer glimpses of interior, and alternative, lives. Like Dada, who must suspect deep down that his appeals to cultural nationalism and familial pride are a thinning mask for his cowardice and his tenuous position within his home and community, George is also anxious about losing his hold over his children and wife. He too is conscious of his precarious position within his neighborhood of Salford, with the Bradford-based Pakistani community, and with his family in Pakistan. The evident turmoil he feels at his children's resistance to traditions that he deems important renders George a much more empathy-inspiring character than Dada. In *A Whistle in the Dark*, the tragic figure more akin to George would be Michael, whose semi-accidental murder of his brother seems to fulfill the living legacy of his father, while his anguish over it and his hopes for that brother suggest a more generous heart. When Mr. Shah, the would-be father-in-law to Abdul and Tariq Khan, makes his first formal visit to the house, the tenuousness of George's control emerges both through their chronic eruptions of rebelliousness and more implicitly in the impossibility of sustaining George's purist vision. George's desire for acceptance within the Pakistani community in Bradford leads him to embrace a paradoxical fusion of materialist social ambition and devout commitment to Islamic religious practices and beliefs. Mr. Shah appears as the standard-bearer of the 'traditions' defined as Pakistani by the social elites of its expatriate community in Bradford. Mr. Shah's enthusiasm for his role as the paragon of Bradford Asian respectability is matched (and possibly surpassed by his complacent pride in his wall-to-wall carpeting and double-glazing. George's position of authority within his home, held more by fear than respect, shifts quickly to one of social inferiority and obsequious deference in the face of the self-satisfied Mr. Shah.

In the preface to his screenplay for the film adaptation of *East Is East*, Khan-Din's explanation of his own father's behavior suggests the autobiographical inspiration for George's characterization:

> I think part of his problem was that he always felt slightly embarrassed by us in the company of his family, who had settled over here... In many ways, he must have felt extremely isolated and would have liked to have lived in a Pakistani community like Bradford.[28]

Khan-Din never shies away from depicting George's tyrannical, violent behavior and its often devastating consequences, but he also allows George's longings and sense of isolation to surface in several quietly moving moments in the play, rendering him a more sympathetic figure. For instance, we see how history's incursions into the Khan's home take a tremendous toll on George, particularly through the family's varying responses the television news features on the independence war in the former East Pakistan. As these broadcasts punctuate the days and nights in the Khan household, George agonizes and fumes over the potential fates of his first wife and family in Azad Kashmir. The Bangladeshi struggle for independence from an increasingly militarized Pakistan parallels the children's conflicts with their authoritarian father. His fears about the impact of border disputes on the security of his Pakistan-based family are matched by fears of the encroaching influences of non-Pakistani social and cultural values on his children. Similarly, his mingled feelings of guilt and relief—guilt for not returning to this family and relief at not living with the struggles and demands of everyday life in Pakistan—hold his feelings for both families in a kind of tension with each other.

This absent family shadows the family that we see on stage. George paints them as both a perfect and a typical Pakistani family: respectful of the patriarch, harmonious, untainted by the "outside" influences he finds so fearsome in England. His views appear to be a source of both comic and real tension for his current wife Ella and most of his English-born children. They are skeptical, even scornful of George's praise for the country and family from which he has been apart for forty years, arguing that such distance lends enchantment, and he and Ella enjoy an ongoing comic banter about his quirks in spite of his temper. The Khans' house is also haunted by the absence of their eldest son, Nazir, disowned by George for resisting the marriage George arranged for him. The family is ordered to treat him as dead, though as Ella tartly observes, "No, he's not, he's living in Eccles [which for some Salford residents might seem a kind of death]. He might be dead to you but he's still my son."[29]

Moments such as these reveal the strengths of Khan-Din's development of those who might otherwise be considered minor characters. Ella, Meenah, and Ella's best friend Annie all display keen senses of humor, independent minds, and strong inclinations to assertiveness (curbed only by George). The sole sister among seven siblings, Meenah is well able to hold her own, even with her elder brothers. Annie, like Ella a native of Salford, possesses both a tremendous compassion for all members of the Khan family, and gift for deflating the pretensions of others. Where Ella's responses to George's behavior are alternately funny and painful but nearly always self-aware, Annie's challenges to George's authority emerge comically and seemingly accidentally. For instance, when Annie pops in at the Khan house to find them entertaining Mr. Shah, she interrupts their discussion of childrearing to praise the Khan children for being 'good Samaritans', provoking a potential crisis with the disapproving Mr. Shah. She echoes Mr. Shah's affirmation of his wife's firm hand with their children by offering her own insight into discipline: "Oh aye, yeah, mind you, our Peter knows how far he can go, before I knock him to kingdom come—and that's just me husband Mr. Shah!"[30] Mr. Shah's characterization hews fairly closely to a caricature of "traditional" Pakistani paternalism mixed with materialism, yet his anxiety over his family's future does inspire mild sympathy. His role as gatekeeper of the community to which George seeks entry ultimately invites us to see him as relatively privileged and powerful, and his willingness to abuse that power to his family's advantage renders him ultimately unsympathetic.

George's aspirations of impressing and ultimately belonging to the Bradford Pakistani community produce some of the funniest moments in the play, even as they demand painful sacrifices from Ella and their seven children. The tensions between George and his children reveal his own conflict within himself over his visions of England and Pakistan. Interestingly, George's authority erodes in one of the few scenes set outside their home. After an embarrassing debacle at the mosque, Ella and George take their youngest son, twelve-year-old Sajit, to be circumcised at the local hospital. When the doctor approaches them after the operation, Ella takes control of the situation, shushing George deprecatingly and urging him to go and call them a taxi while she talks to the doctor. Her strictness with Sajit and George derives from a parallel desire for social acceptance: "I'm not having my kids being accused of bad manners. People are a lot quicker to point the finger if they see they're a bit foreign."[31] Here her behavior is more assertive—and George's more passive—than in their home. These scenes suggest that George has had a succession of disempowering experiences—as a target for both English racism and Pakistani racism and elitism—resulting from his marriage to Ella and choice of Salford as home as well as from his decision to raise his children as Muslims. In this respect, they suggest more complex sources or triggers of his insecurity and rage.

As his exclusionary and racist treatment in England is internalized, George's reaction is to embrace more conservative Pakistani and Muslim values than he might have done had he remained in Pakistan or found England a less hostile environment. Thus, the household has become George's domain through a combination of threatened and actual violence and the tactical concessions of his wife Ella and their children. Constantly living under the cloud of "what Dad did to Mam last time", which emerges implicitly as his near-fatal beating of her after Nazir fled the house, the children must negotiate their lives outside of the house around their parents' strict demands of their time and behavior. Ella mediates between a kind of conspiratorial complicity with her children, for instance by allowing Salim to secretly study art instead of engineering or warning Abdul and Tariq that their father is planning their engagements, and a submission to the often tyrannical will of George, as with her concession to twelve-year-old Sajit's circumcision and to Nazir's banishment from their home after his rebellion. The flow of action through the space of the set illustrates the numerous codes and nuances by which Ella and the children can gauge George's moods and circumvent his authority. George's impending entry into the house frequently precipitates a flurry of covert activity, as the children hide the evidence of their sausage eating, or son Salim's art portfolio, or anything else forbidden by their father. As George struggles to gain social acceptance for his family within the Pakistani community in Bradford, he becomes an outsider in his own house. The conflicts are well framed by the set design and the first scene. The split set contains the house and the chip shop owned by George and Ella. Two rooms and a kitchen with an outside shed comprise the house. From the laundry piled on the Lazy Susan on their kitchen table to the overall set décor, it is clear that the family lives in very tight quarters, but also that they have made an effort to make the rooms presentable.

Khan-Din's play borders on the farcical (although not as broadly so as its 1999 film adaptation) in its depiction of the simultaneous pull of Pakistan, Salford, and Bradford on the family. Packed with verbal and visual comedy, the play also brings to life the confusion, conflict and violence that form part of their domestic life. George, the patriarch of the Khan family in *East Is East* maintains a similarly physically violent and authoritarian grip on his family, but with considerably less malevolence and self-glorification than Dada Carney. Upon leaving Pakistan in the 1930s, George also left a first wife and children, with whom he remains in contact, sending goods and money to them from England. His sense of obligation, perhaps based on feelings of guilt, produce a strong sense of affiliation to his home state of Azad Kashmir. The tensions between George and his children reveal his own conflict within himself over his visions of England and Pakistan. In their efforts to assert control over their family within these environments, George and Dada similarly struggle against their own sense of disorientation and inner conflict. Both men find it too difficult to face their incompatibility with the Ireland and the Pakistan that they nostalgically invoke, and impossible to accept the changes that life in England might demand of themselves and their families.

The ending of *A Whistle in the Dark* suggests a far bleaker outlook for any accommodation within England or Ireland for the remaining Carneys, with the death of Des and the departure of Betty. Dada no longer casts a spell over the brothers, who are now symbolically more closely bonded with Michael.

However, the familial belonging that emerges through their isolation from both communities is more a form of imprisonment than a source of security or comfort. Not only is Dada unable to sustain his vision of belonging and heroism through his sons, but they can no longer sustain their self-image through him. Michael's act of violence and Dada's response has the perverse effect of releasing the brothers from their father's hold over them, much as Blake's murder of Dinny in *The Walworth Farce* potentially frees his brother Sean from the confinement imposed by their father. Both plays' endings, however, suggest only the slightest of hopes for the sons' future prospects.

These fathers' struggles to assert their authority through a familial and cultural mythology finds very different means of expression in these plays, from farce to tragedy. Yet the plays' portrayals of these struggles and these mythologies illuminate the ways that the colonial relations of Ireland and Pakistan to Britain have informed their versions of migrant masculinity. These plays introduce the possibility of restructuring these familial orders and of establishing new identities and communal relationships. The ending of *East Is East* suggests this might involve a more positive transformation for the family, in which the children and Ella begin to change the dynamic in their household in a way that might be sustainable. They find a way to protect her and themselves, and to reconcile their conflicting familial, social, and personal demands.

Khan-Din's dramatic reconstruction of his family life amidst a neighborhood and community now dismantled and dissolved (except in memory) suggests the compassionate hindsight (rather than nostalgia) of a writer who has found such reconciliation. In many respects, both of these plays evoke an (offstage) England of postwar deprivation and cultural polarities that late 1990s audiences, in the midst of a British mania for Asian culture, might have placed elsewhere and in the past. In more recent recessionary and volatile times, with Asian migrant and minority families in Britain continuing to suffer racialized assault and harassment, profiling and surveillance (both official and unofficial), and highly publicized accounts of patriarchal violence, such dramatizations of Asian migrant and minority masculinities might carry more currency. Many more recent productions, including *The Walworth Farce*, illuminate how the polarized identifications and intimately-lived or internalized cultural conflicts of Irish and Asian migrants and their families persist well beyond the periods and places of *A Whistle in the Dark* and *East Is East*.

Chapter Five

DIFFERENT FOR GIRLS

> I look after. I take care. I do all that. For nothing. I'm not home care, I'm just a person. And if I can do it for her, I'll do it for myself.
>
> Gurpreet Kaur Bhatti, *Behzti*

One critical task of this book has been to examine how imperialism and its legacies have shaped the stories of immigration and British cultural identity from multiple perspectives. While this chapter sustains this postcolonial critical approach, it shifts its focus from the politics of masculinity to the gender dynamics for female characters and theater artists. Gender oppression has long been implicated in the politics of both colonialism and anticolonialism, in ways both explicitly and implicitly addressed by writers. Indebted to the critical work of Susan Croft, Gabriele Griffin, Christiane Schlote, and Giovanna Buonanno, and others who have written extensively on British South Asian and Black British women playwrights, this analysis introduces an additional diasporic cultural perspective, that of Irish female migrants in Britain.[1] Contemporary popular culture and media images of women migrants from these regions and their daughters often stereotype them as devout, submissive, and uneducated, and their source countries as anti-modern, repressive, and violent. In her analysis of Meera Syal's *My Sister-Wife*, May Joseph offers a reading of such images as not entirely false but rather as elements of a range of competing mythologies:

> With great wit, Syal sketches the tortuous and circumlocutory ways through which immigrants in Britain negotiate between the customary traditions of former homelands and the less evident, more contemporary orthodoxies of the secular culture within which they must live as British subjects.[2]

Joseph uses "customary traditions of former homelands" to refer to a range of cultural and religious practices that immigrants might sustain through journeys to and from their home countries, or may remember from their own immediate past, or might find imposed by other members of their diasporic community. As the quote suggests, such traditions often emerge in these works as at odds with the host culture and its own invocations of order, progress, and secularism. What audiences might learn from these works is that even where such dichotomies might be sought and found, the characters' perspectives and stories differ profoundly, even for migrants within the same family. The comparative focus on Caribbean, Irish and Asian migration in the works treated in this chapter reveals connections in their dramatizations of familial dynamics, of religious institutions and practices, and of their intersections. In foregrounding female migrant and minority subjectivities, the plays illuminate the ways in which these women encounter or hold patriarchal and colonial expectations for themselves and for others.

In many of the plays discussed earlier in this book, the male characters' internal and interpersonal struggles constitute the core conflicts of their respective works and are given greater dramatic weight than those of the female characters. Edgar White's Irene and Sabena Williams, Mustapha Matura's Batee, and Tom Murphy's Mrs. Carneys (Michael's wife Betty and his offstage, unnamed mother) are either peripheral to the play's drama or entirely invisible, even when they serve as foils or catalysts for their male counterparts' actions. While most of these playwrights sustain this tight focus on the male migrant's perspective, some nevertheless create complex and often sympathetic female migrant characters. Nigel Moffat's *Mamma Decemba* represents one such figure, as her titular character is often the sole presence on stage, and her struggles and voice form the dramatic core of the play. Michael Abbensetts' Rita Fletcher offers brief glimpses into an interior life of a wife and mother, but it is her husband Tony whose desires and actions drive the play. Khan-Din's Ella Khan is a multidimensional character whose scenes with her best friend in *East is East* reveal both a local and a personal history that defines her independently of her husband and children. Like her children, she is born in Britain, but unlike them, she is white and not marked as an outsider in Salford in the way that George or her children might be. Khan-Din's other work has also featured some sympathetically drawn, complex women and girls, with some insight into their perspectives. Ella Khan also evokes an earlier playwright's creation, Helen in Shelagh Delaney's debut play *A Taste of Honey*. Like Ella, Helen is Salford-born, but as a working-class single mother living on the fringes of her society, Helen's character was a rare appearance on the 1950s stage. Where Helen is rootless and keen on self-preservation, Ella is firmly rooted in her communal and familial relationships, constantly (and visibly) struggling to do what she thinks is best for her family. Delaney's 1958 play marked one of the first collaborations between a female director, Joan Littlewood and a young female playwright, and is also notable for its portrayal of an interracial sexual relationship and of white British ignorance of the lives of Black British. In this play, Helen's daughter Jo assumes that her dark-skinned suitor and father of her child is an African prince or an exotic migrant, rather than the Cardiff-born sailor he turns out to be.

Discussing the plays that form the basis for her book *Black and Asian Women Playwrights in Britain* (2003), Gabriele Griffin identifies their common elements:

> ...its thematic concerns often centre on questions of female agency, the status of women within their communities both historically and currently, mother-daughter relationships, female friendship, domestic violence, [...] and last but not least, female experiences of migration. As such it validates or recognizes Black and Asian women's experience and cultural presence in a medium—theatre—still [...] very much dominated by white middle-class values and audiences.[3]

Griffin expands on these thematic concerns in her analysis of the plays, but first outlines what she views as a thematic shift in much of the writing of Black and Asian women playwrights, from the intergenerational conflicts between migrant parent and "migrated" children that formed the core of many plays of the 1980s to a focus in the plays of the 1990s on the issues linked to living in contemporary Britain as part of a generation that has grown up in the UK.[4] For both generations, finding "home" carries tremendous importance, even if its definition and location might widely differ. For some migrant parents, "home" is an abandoned or deferred goal, something given up in the hope that their children will find greater opportunities for success. For some of their British-born children, "home" is elsewhere as well, defined as a space of belonging in opposition to the feelings of alienation triggered by the marginalization they might experience.

Through their focus on immigrant women and their struggles to adapt to living in Britain, and their daughters' efforts to find their own space within their country of birth, some of the plays examined here illuminate the ways migration both expands and shrinks their worlds. While central to and often driving the action of the play, most of these female migrant characters identify primarily as mothers. The plays typically depict them as overwhelmingly concerned with the material welfare of their family and the education of their children, which they regard as a critical means of achieving better conditions and lives for the next generation than they have experienced themselves. With these priorities in mind, they often sacrifice any possibilities for their own happiness or self-development, and impose strict control over their children's behavior and use of time. Ann Devlin's *After Easter* (1995) and Gurpreet Kaur Bhatti's *Behzti* (2004) depict the struggles for women migrants across generations to find their place in British society, as well as in the families that they inherit or those they try to make. These two plays along with Mary O'Malley's *Once a Catholic* all suggest the ways patriarchal authority, classism, and corruption intertwine in the institutions in which these families invest their hopes and faith.

Many of these plays simultaneously depict the perspectives of the daughters of these migrants and their efforts to accommodate or resist parental and other expectations and control of their lives. This control takes different forms from that exerted on their sons—with access to knowledge of the world and their dress, behavior, and sexual desire (or potential promiscuity) being the recurring foci of parental concern. In challenging or defying their parents, these daughters make themselves vulnerable to an often pitiless and exploitative society that imposes its own demands upon them. Conversely, any rewards held out to them, whether financial or emotional, often depend on their ability to please their male partners and families, or to fulfill the expectations held of dutiful daughters and wives. With no direct connection to their parents' countries of birth, and often facing discrimination and assumptions of their foreignness in Britain, these native-born British experience their own forms of displacement and alienation.

Social/Sexual Trauma and the Pressure to Be "a Good Girl"

Most of the plays that feature female migrants and second-generation migrant characters share a preoccupation with the ways material needs or even values overtake emotional and spiritual ones. The immigrant mothers in these plays place high value on hard work and financial security, often at the expense of their personal lives, and seem to work from a desire to see their daughters *not* replicate their lives. The fathers in these plays, where they appear at all, seem anxious to preserve their daughters' marriageability and want to see their aspirations for social acceptance—with heavy emphasis on conservative cultural values—fulfilled through their daughters' lives and marriages. Depictions of Asian fathers in the plays are particularly emphatic about this, though it is often also incumbent on (and in some cases even the impetus of) the mothers in the families to reinforce these values for the next generation. Such conditions seem to persist into the age of texting and Google, as vigilant families can stifle these young women's access to such means of communication and information and some of the characters can be self secluding. These conditions can even persist into adulthood for women whose circumstances have hindered them from developing a social life.

For instance, in Bhatti's *Behtzi*, which depicts a rape that takes place in a Sikh temple, the victim, Min, is a thirty-something innocent whose life has been narrowly circumscribed by her duties to her ailing mother Balbir, by an ever watchful and judgmental community, and by her own insecurities about her body and sexuality. Her dancing, one physical pleasure in which she shyly but enthusiastically indulges in the semi-privacy of the home she shares with her mother, is ridiculed by Balbir, who regards her daughter as an unattractive and unlikely prospective bride for any suitor. Not only do her mother's and her own anxieties repress Min's sensual self, but her spiritual longings are belittled as well. Her vision of the gurdwara (Sikh temple) as a safe space is dismissed by her mother as a romantic notion, and it becomes clear later in the play that her mother may have been speaking from both experience of and insight into the ways material ambition and carnal desires are at work in their gurdwara. Min's brutal rape by the family friend and community "fixer," who directs the temple's affairs, is at first unrecognized by her mother and condoned by the "aunties" in the interests of social and material ambition, competition with each other, and the belief that the younger generation of women must "suffer as we did." As Gabriele Griffin describes it,

> Mothers, disappointed with the lives of maldistribution and misrecognition they have been forced to live, seek continuity of their dreams and hopes through the lives they want their daughters to lead, unwilling to recognize that the daughters live under conditions that—although still based on misrecognition and the unequal distribution of resources—put into question the values that the mothers embrace.[5]

However, Min's mother Balbir has a transformative experience, shifting within this scene from forcing her daughter to submit to brutal treatment to becoming her champion and bucking the patriarchal power structure of the temple and community. At the same time, she holds classist and racist attitudes towards well-meaning "outsiders" such as the caregiver who loves and values Min in ways the others seem unable to.[6] Mr. Sandhu, a powerful fixer to whom the women turn for marriage prospects for their daughters and contracts for their sons, maintains a public persona that enables him to exploit young women while purportedly upholding the honor and values deemed central to Sikh culture. In this play, Balbir begins to question these values after she sees their hollowness, not necessarily through a rejection of the abuse of Min for its own sake, but through her realization that what she viewed as a necessary act will yield them nothing in the way of social or material security.

The play's 2004 reception reveals similarly complex forms of silencing and solidarity, as some representatives of the Birmingham Sikh community (others defended the play) called on the play's producing theatre, Birmingham Repertory Theatre, to cancel the production, with some protesters storming the theatre on its opening night and breaking windows and making threats against the theater's staff and the playwright, and causing the theatre to cancel the production.[7] Bhatti's reactions to the threats on her life were to go into hiding, acknowledging the danger she faced, and to continue to write plays. Her most recent plays, *Behud* ("without limits") and *AD2050* both address religious extremism and hypocrisy in differing contexts. The former play addresses the crisis around *Behzti* with the playwright as a central character, and had its premiere in 2010 with no incident at the Belgrade Theatre in Coventry. *AD2050*, produced by Kali Theatre Company, is set in a futuristic London altered by climate change and absolutist religious law, from which the characters are attempting to escape to the liberal oasis of Istanbul. Bhatti's response to attempted silencing and censorship relies on sharp satire and defiance.

Mary O'Malley's *Once a Catholic* (1978) caused a furor of lesser proportion for its chapel scene featuring the attachment of a wax penis to the figure of Christ by a schoolgirl.[8] The play offers a satirical view of the individual plights of the many Marys that make up one class in a north London Catholic school. Second-generation immigrants for the most part, each Mary embodies a different mix of sexual curiosity or prurience, social anxiety, rebelliousness, and familial loyalty. The play comically sends up the "moral education" provided by the parochial schools industry (the roll call of Marys underscores this depiction of convent school as a kind of factory for "good" Catholic wives, mothers, nurses or nuns). Set in 1950s London, *Once a Catholic* does not specifically address immigration, but the displacement of the girls' immigrant families is recounted through their exchanges with each other and their teachers. Sexual repression on the institutional and familial level is seen through the girls' behavior towards each other (and revelations of parents' statements and activities) and in their altercations with teachers. We never see the parents in this play. Instead we watch the girls fumble through their world, naively engaging in teenage and adult experiences as they display varying degrees of rebelliousness and innocence. The play centers its action on the school and the homes of the two young male characters. Thus, the girls' dialogue and interactions in these spaces conjures their unseen familial lives and homes and establishes a tension between the ever present, ever watchful teachers and the often invoked but unseen parents.

The more recent plays *Speechless* (Shared Experience, 2010) and *Fragile Land* (2003) depict young women in the grip of societal and parental values, with the former's migrant family upholding an idealized image of the imperial "family" (as embodied, as Yasmin Alibhai-Brown argues, in the televised wedding of the virginal Diana to Prince Charles), and in the latter by the conservative patriarchal values of the adolescent Tasleema's father. Hindu, Christian, and Muslim patriarchal values come under scrutiny through the girls' resistance not only to their parents' control, but to also that of the young men and others driven by their own varying interests to "help" the girls. The plays also poignantly capture the adolescent tug of loyalties amongst sisters and friends and between a sense of familial and institutional duty and a desire for wider experience of the world. *Fragile Land's* Tasleema and Lux, from different religious and ethnic backgrounds, share concerns about the parental and peer pressures that they face, even while differing in their affinities for and responses to those they encounter in their lives outside of the home. In this respect, they resemble the girls of Our Lady of Fatima, the Mathews sisters in *Leavetaking,* or the twins in *Speechless,* each of whom struggles to reconcile who they are perceived to be (both within and outside of their family) with who they want or aspire to be.

Speechless is the work of the feminist theater company Shared Experience, which is known for its expressionist productions of literary works such as *Jane Eyre* and of plays such as *The House of Bernarda Alba.* Longtime Shared Experience playwright Polly Teale worked with Linda Brogan to adapt Marjorie Wallace's nonfiction account of twins June and Jennifer Gibbons, daughters of Barbadian immigrants. Their refusal to speak to adults and development of their own private language led to their isolation and marginalization, their traumatic separation and adolescent delinquency, and then to their incarceration in Broadmoor. On their release in 1993, at the age of thirty, Jennifer Gibbons died in transit from the hospital. Both avid writers, June has had her fiction published and has given several public interviews since her sister's death. Yasmin Alibhai-Brown describes the Gibbons' story as a "parable" of the postwar Caribbean migrants' encounter with "Mother England." In her foreword, she discusses how these migrants coped (or did not) with the disillusionment borne of their discovery that their inculcation in British values and service to the empire/nation did not shield them from a hostile and racist reception. "For a minority disillusionment led to anger which was either internalized—leading to mental chaos—or externalized, acted out in crimes and acts of destruction. In the Gibbons family, you witness the range from denial to destruction. The father, mother and children incarnate the different reactions, as characters do on stage in the great tragedies."[9] *Speechless* deals with the adolescent sexuality of the Gibbons twins and the racist bullying they experience as schoolgirls. The predatory nature of school comes through in both plays, as does the fact that girls are branded as vulnerable, misfits, and thus targeted by class bullies. In *Once a Catholic*, this preying upon the weak and vulnerable is not merely an activity of the schoolchildren, but also of the nuns, priests, and the institutions themselves.

These plays connect through their concern with the internalization of gender roles and the demonization of female expression of sexuality, anger, rebellion, or independence. These women often police themselves and each other nearly as much as they are controlled and policed by the institutions and male figures in their lives, and occasionally more so. In the schools, homes, and other private and public spaces that constitute the settings of *Once a Catholic*, *Fragile Land*, and *Speechless*, the female characters are under myriad forms of surveillance and are often shown to be the objects of mistaken assumptions based on seemingly direct observation. There are different, but in many ways deeply connected challenges for the women of *After Easter* and *Behzti*, in that we see how aspects of their childhood or repressed parts of themselves return to haunt or harm them as adults. The plays suggest or explicitly show how these immigrant women and their children are particularly vulnerable to violence, isolation, confinement, and control. In her analysis of realist and nonrealist techniques in *After Easter*, Enrica Cerquoni contrasts slice-of-life-realism with this play's approach, arguing that this play instead emphasizes the "the drama of the invisible."[10] Cerquoni argues that Greta's task involves remaking her inhabited space "into a lived space of consciousness," and goes on to explain that for Greta, "this 'unmarked' status of free-floating is marked in the stage directions as 'home' for Greta. In the plurality of her fractured selves, which have been given expression through emotional, spiritual, and psychic images, voices and other characters' experiences, the female protagonist finds the 'inner room' she has sought for so long."[11] In some ways, her preoccupations with and approaches to consciousness, identity, memory, and history connect her to Dublin-based playwright Sebastian Barry, whose characters experience comparable forms of exile without ever leaving Ireland. Whether using the spaces of the stage in realist or nonrealist ways, these plays push their audiences to recognize the ways in which institutions and individuals assert their control over female perspectives, voices, and bodies.

Griffin makes an interesting claim for the potentially radical intervention made by dramatic work that follows conventional forms such as naturalism or realism, listing their five key functions:

> First, it places Black and Asian women's theatre work within a recognizable theatrical frame, thus staking its claim for recognition within that convention rather than as part of the traditions of a (post)colonial other. Secondly, it forces the recognition that Black and Asian playwrights born and brought up in Britain relate to the theatre work conducted in the UK rather than, or at least as much as, to the performance traditions that might dominate the countries from which their parents or grandparents came. Thirdly, it articulates a demand for the recognition of issues faced by Black and Asian communities in Britain as issues to be addressed, not least in high cultural, public forms, and sites. Fourthly, it demands recognition of the material realities within which Black and Asian women's lives are played out. And finally, it refuses the transformation of the issues Black and Asian women face in the UK into purely aesthetic projects.[12]

Griffin's argument echoes elements of Patricia Schroeder's claims for the potential usefulness of realism. While her book examines feminist American drama from the early twentieth century, Schroeder's acknowledgment of contemporary feminist critiques of realism that argue it reinforces patriarchal familial values through plots that subordinate female characters is worth noting with respect to postwar British drama as well. She cites an additional critique of realism from an African-American perspective, which finds that realism's reality claims exclude various invisible elements, such as ghosts, ancestors, and historical figures or conditions (which echoes Enrica Cerquoni's critique of realism as not allowing for "the drama of the invisible"), but then proposes that realism not be viewed as a static point in a linear evolutionary trajectory from realism to antirealism.[13] We might read productions that integrate female diasporic perspectives into realist forms as claiming a central place for these subjects within a dominant British dramatic tradition.

Griffin's book focuses on the challenge for Black and Asian women of achieving "cultural visibility," a challenge that Jatinder Verma identifies as an essential response to both invisibility and the vulnerability that comes with a visibility imposed through profiling, stereotyping, harassment and other formal and informal practices of surveillance that British Asians encounter. Griffin argues that these women writers face a triple challenge of racism, sexism, and classism, whether in finding the conditions and opportunities to write, getting their work produced, and having that produced work studied, reviewed, or even acknowledged. Irish and Irish British women face different forms of marginalization with respect to this triple challenge and in terms of their visibility versus invisibility. Nevertheless, the work of women playwrights from Mary O'Malley to Ann Devlin to the Belfast-based Marie Jones illuminates multiple forms of racism, classism, and sexism encountered by migrant and second-generation Irish women in Britain.

Irish male migrants are much more "visible" on British stages, in the works of Kavanagh, O'Casey, and Friel as well as those treated in the previous chapters. One could argue that the works of Enda Walsh, Tom Murphy, and Jimmy Murphy present their almost exclusively male worlds and their characters' conflicts as indictments of the patriarchal values of both Irish and British societies. Martin McDonagh and Conor McPherson offer sympathetic portrayals of the conditions of migration—both internal and external—for Irish women, in McDonagh's title character of *The Beauty Queen of Leenane*, Maureen Folan, and in McPherson's Valerie, the "blow-in" of *The Weir* who moves from Dublin to a rural Irish village. Their experiences of migration do not form the center of the play, but they do offer sharp insight into the vulnerability and anguish that can accompany such dislocation. Maureen's description of her time cleaning offices in England and the sole exchange of kindness she experienced with another female cleaner from the Caribbean reveals unseen dimensions to her character that go unrecognized by those closest to her. While a history of relative privilege within the colonial racial hierarchy might divide Irish from Caribbean women, the shared experiences of hostility and poverty in post-imperial Britain seems to inspire a postcolonial solidarity between Maureen and her co-worker.

In a very different style, *The Weir* exposes the tensions and affinities between the members of a community through scenes that take place entirely within a local pub, where Valerie is the sole woman and sole non-local in the gathering. The play suggests the ways in which Ireland's tourist economy has both internal and external dimensions, with Valerie's relative affluence marking her as a privileged outsider. In a round of initially light-hearted storytelling about local ghosts and fairies, Valerie shares her own ghost story, of her child's death and her experiences of a form of post-death communication with the child. Her vulnerability and visible grief sparks a change in the dynamics of privilege and deprivation, outsider and insider, and of guarded courtesy and intimacy within the group.

The pub is a common setting for much modern Irish drama, and has come to feature more frequently in contemporary British drama, both as a gathering spot for Irish exiles such as the men of Jimmy Murphy's *Kings of the Kilburn High Road*, or for the white and Black British football fans of Roy Williams's *Sing Yer Heart Out For the Lads*. These and other pubs often function as spaces where gender roles and local and national identities are contested. Vulnerability and visibility are not typically rewarded in the ways that Valerie's experience suggests, and verbal and physical aggression features much more often. In the latter play, Gina, the female owner-manager of the pub, must assert herself with her family and clients in an increasingly racially polarized and emotionally charged context, and she struggles to balance the need to maintain order in her pub with the desire to sustain her relationships. The pub figures symbolically as the nation as the characters fight over its boundaries and its ownership, drawing and redrawing lines of belonging and exclusion in their speech and actions. This pub/nation is both raced and gendered in myriad ways, for instance as Gina's rights as proprietor are continually challenged by her father and son, as well as by a customer who looks askance at her past romance with a black man. Gina asserts her own authority within the pub by physically threatening a young black classmate of her son's, who has been bullying him, and then by appealing to the police to have his mother arrested when she comes to protest his treatment. This subplot reveals the ways female resistance to patriarchal control can be displaced by white female privilege when the circumstances shift.

Both the promises and perils of recognition and visibility for women both on and off the stage continue to be a concern for scholars and practitioners of theater, and Griffin's book represents an important contribution to feminist and theater studies for its critical analysis of the particular challenges facing Black and Asian women playwrights, and of the diverse thematic and formal approaches of their work. For its breadth of topics, the book delves deeply into its postcolonial and diasporic theoretical analysis of the plays and their production and reception histories. Such demands involve more than character development and thematic focus, however, and Griffin further argues:

> Discussions about how to achieve (social) justice utilized different models of how to understand the causes of injustice, arguing on the one hand that injustice was due to the unequal distribution of resources, therefore requiring redistribution, and on the other, that injustice was a function of the lack of recognition of and respect for differences between diverse groups of people, therefore requiring recognition.[14]

Beginning in the 1980s, many Black and Asian female theatre artists sought such redistribution of resources and recognition by founding their own theater companies, companies that commissioned plays by and about diverse women, and nurtured the development of women's careers in all areas of theatre production, from writing to design to directing. These artists do cite the Black Theatre Co-Operative, Tara Arts, and the Temba Theatre Company as male-led companies that provided crucial opportunities for Black and Asian actresses to play central and multidimensional roles. Further, several productions by these companies engaged in a feminist historiography or provided sympathetic portrayals of underrepresented women's struggles. Tara Arts engaged in the former in *Scenes in the Life* (based on Amrit Wilson's 1978 account of conditions for Asian women in Britain) and in the latter with *Playing the Flame*, and Black Theatre Co-Operative produced Jacqueline Rudet's *Money to Live*, about prostitution. Nevertheless, a growing number of female theatre artists sought to expand the range and depth of roles for themselves both on and off stage.

Street view of Tara Arts Theatre Company building in Earlsfield, London—
the company's home for the past thirty years.
(Photo courtesy of Artistic Director Jatinder Verma.)

Many of these women found each other in workshops, youth theatre, conservatories, and college theater departments that were growing more culturally diverse. What they found when they emerged from their programs and schools was a theatrical world that wanted to pigeonhole them. In founding and running these companies, they had to be resourceful in building the professional and institutional relationships that would sustain their creative aspirations beyond the commissioning and casting criteria of a largely white, male, middle-class theater establishment. Many of these figures recognized that what was needed for more women to succeed was training, resources, and opportunities, if not the theatrical equivalent of "a room of one's own." While the 1980s proved to be a watershed decade for Black British writing and for the founding of theater companies, several migrant women who worked in performing arts in earlier decades offered both exemplary and cautionary lessons for these younger artists.

Some migrant women of the early postwar generation who worked in theater, such as Jamila Massey or Pearl Connor Mogotsi (then Pearl Connor), found an active intellectual community of musicians, politicians, lawyers, activists, and artists, through which they were able to work in venues in London from television programs to the Players Theatre, and at festivals in various towns around the country.[15] Una Marson, the Jamaican poet, arrived in 1932 as an already published poet, and was the first Black woman to be employed by the BBC, where she worked on several series ("Calling the West Indies" and another series with George Orwell) before launching her own poetry program for them called "Caribbean Voices." It was on this program that English audiences would be introduced to the work and voice of Samuel Selvon, Andrew Salkey, Derek Walcott, and many others. Indian-born actress Jamila Massey arrived in the UK as a child and worked from an early age on BBC Radio acting in children's programs. She went on to complete her university degree and put her language and acting skills to work for the BBC in radio and television, rounding out a career in film and theater with recurring roles on the popular radio series *The Archers* and the television series *East Enders*. Pearl Connor's husband Edric Connor was the first Black actor to appear in Stratford, in a 1958 production of *Pericles* directed by Tony Richardson. Having come to Britain to study law, Connor-Mogotsi became involved in theater through Edric, and then went on to start an agency for Black theater artists, working with such actors as Corinne Skinner, Mona Hammond, Suzy Wong, Ram John Holder. She cites her Trinidadian background as enabling her to work well with African and Asian diasporic actors.[16]

Indian-born actress Alaknanda Samarth moved to Britain from the US after completing university there and earning a scholarship to the Royal Academy of Dramatic Art, where she enrolled in 1960. She found work on television more than in theater in Britain, in spite of having acted professionally in India in a range of plays from the western canon. Samarth continued to act in television and theater in Britain and in film and theater in India, moving between these two countries and then spending a brief period living in Africa. She reflects on her career as an actress as an effort to find a means of evoking spirit, language and cultural memory both from within and without the cultures in which she works, and argues that sustaining this "confluence of cultures" as hybridity rather than as adaptation is "what produces the most powerful art."[17]

Yvonne Brewster arrived in London from Jamaica in the mid-1950s, studying both theatre and music (at Rose Bruford College and the Royal Academy of Music, respectively). She claims to be the first Black drama student in Britain,[18] before returning to Jamaica to found the Barn, a theater company based in Kingston. She returned to England in the 1980s and worked in radio and television before co-founding the Talawa Theatre Company. Like Samarth, Brewster has managed to sustain theatrical careers (and companies) in her two "homes." Brewster co-founded Talawa Theatre Company with the actresses Mona Hammond and Carmen Monroe, and the designer Inigo Espejel in 1985 to produce work of male and female playwrights of the African diaspora. Among their productions are British premieres of Ola Rotimi's *The Gods Are Not to Blame* and Dennis Scott's *An Echo in the Bone,* as well as London premieres of work by Derek Walcott and Wole Soyinka. Talawa has also produced several new writing festivals featuring short plays by Black British writers. The company, which derives its name from the Jamaican dialect term meaning "feisty," has had both male and female artistic directors since Brewster retired in 2003.

Brewster's was not an expressly feminist agenda, in fact she explains to Lizbeth Goodman that being raised in a matriarchal (Jamaican) society formed her approach to theatre differently from her feminist contemporaries in Britain.[19] Yet at the same time, she states that she and her co-founders were seeking to present work "from a woman's perspective" but were unable to commission new plays for budgetary reasons.[20] Brewster discussed the dearth of Jamaican women playwrights and the difficulties of finding the work of those that have written in an interview for the BBC Radio 4 program "Woman's Hour" in 2012. Asked about choosing the works for her newly published collection of three Jamaican plays for the fiftieth anniversary of Jamaican independence (in which two of the plays are by women), Brewster goes on to tell Aasmah Mir that she found the same challenge in the UK when running Talawa, namely that she struggled to find plays by Black women to produce.[21] As she told Lizbeth Goodman earlier (in the 1996 interview), "We have always wanted to produce plays by women, but during the first few years we had difficulty in finding appropriate plays by a woman.... We needed epic plays."[22] Nevertheless, the company has nurtured new drama by Black British women (Dona Daley, Faith Miller) through newer projects such as its Black Women Writers project (funded by the London Arts Board) and has worked with many female directors. Talawa's current Artistic Director, Michael Buffong, kicked off his tenure in early 2012 with a series titled "Talawa Firsts," which featured five new Black British plays, most of which were written and/or directed by women. Talawa was one of the only companies to realize its dream of finding a theatrical home for itself in a building-based theatre. Though its residence in the Cochrane Theatre lasted only three years and was a rental arrangement, Brewster argues that it showed both the benefits of having a stable base from which to work as a company, while also revealing the limitations of renting such a base and having no ultimate control over the overall programming and design of the space.[23]

Talawa, Tamasha, and Kali have been the longest lasting of these female-founded companies, and both Tamasha and Kali continue to be run by women. Several other companies as well were at one point or remain vital generators of new dramatic work and of transformative roles for women, both on and off the stage. For instance, Theatre of Black Women (founded by Bernadine Evaristo, Paulette Randall, and Patricia Hilaire in 1982), produced many notable plays by female playwrights. Black Women's Theatre Group similarly identifies itself as promoting work by Black women, and as explicitly feminist.[24] Jacqueline Rudet was an early example, founding her theater company, Imani Faith, in 1983. A veteran of women's and socialist theater companies, Rudet set up the company to promote Black women's writing. The company did not last long, but she continued to write for the theatre. Other playwrights to emerge during this period were Meera Syal, Tanika Gupta, Jackie Kay, Trish Cooke, and Sudha Bhuchar.

Sudha Bhuchar and director Kristine Landon-Smith founded Tamasha Theatre Company in 1989, also working with male and female playwrights and also without an expressed focus on women's lives or feminist ideals. Women artists have worked in all areas of the company from writing to production design to direction to marketing; in recent years, Kristine Landon-Smith has worked in partnership with Tamasha's longtime designer, Sue Mayes, to introduce an initiative that offers designers and directors an opportunity to explore the collaborative relationship through a hands-on intensive course called Design Direct. Many of Tamasha's works focus sharply on women's working and domestic lives in India, Pakistan, and the UK. Their early play *Women of the Dust* drew from interviews and oral histories about women construction workers in India and was commissioned by Oxfam for its 50th anniversary commemoration. Jamila Massey was part of the cast of this play. In 2010, Sudha Bhuchar adapted Federico Garcia Lorca's *The House of Bernarda Alba* for Tamasha. *The House of Bilquis Bibi* featured a cast of nine women, and an inventive translation of the tragedy from early twentieth-century Spain to a present-day Punjabi village setting. The cover of this book features an image commissioned for Tamasha's 2013 premiere of *The Arrival*. Co-creators Kristine Landon-Smith and Sita Brahmachari collaborated with London's Circus Space to adapt Shaun Tan's graphic novel that depicts one immigrant's journey. Other recent work by Tamasha has included *Sweet Cider* by Emteaz Hussain, an outgrowth of Tamasha's new writing program that premiered at Arcola Theatre, a Hackney-based company and arts venue founded in 2000 by Turkish-born director Mehmet Ergen.

Rita Wolf and Rukhsana Ahmad's founding of Kali in 1990 was with a more explicitly feminist purpose, as evidenced by the company's self-description:

> Kali is the UK's only theatre company dedicated to championing women writers from a South Asian background. We seek out original writers who challenge our perceptions. We focus on content and ideas as much as on style to present memorable theatre based on challenging and innovative ideas. No idea is too small, no statement too large. We actively encourage our writers and audience to reinvent and reshape the theatrical agenda.[25]

Kali's claims to recognition and redistribution of artistic resources for South Asian women writers are clear and persuasive. Recent productions have continued to nurture the work of writers addressing past and current challenges of immigration to Britain. These include Sonia Likhari's *Behna* (2010), which takes place (and premiered) in an actual kitchen (actually presented in four kitchens in Birmingham and nearby towns), Sonali Bhattacharya's *A Thin Red Line* (2007, an outgrowth of community workshops held in the Black Country and Birmingham), Azma Dar's *Paper Thin* (2006), and Yasmin Whittaker Khan's *Bells* (2005), among many other works, typically developed from staged readings to full productions. In their writing programs description, Kali emphasizes this commitment, stating that "[s]upporting Asian Women to write for the theatre lies at the core of all that Kali does. All of our projects seek to support, encourage and promote new theatre writing by Asian women."[26]

The work of these theatre companies participates in a larger stream of work by female playwrights or feminist theatre companies in postwar Britain. Women's theatre or feminist theatre companies such as Women's Theatre Group (which changed its name to The Sphinx in 1992), Clean Break, Shared Experience and Monstrous Regiment have all been prolific producers of new writing by women for the theater. By the 1980s and 1990s, these companies were producing works about displacement in the lives of Caribbean and Black British women by playwrights Winsome Pinnock and Jenny McLeod, among others. Work such as Pinnock's *Mules* (Clean Break, 1995), Trish Cooke's *Running Dream* (Second Wave, 1989; Theatre Royal Stratford East, 1993), and Cooke's *Back Street Mammy* (Temba, 1989).

Where female theatre artists of Asian and Caribbean background initially found it nearly impossible to break into mainstream theatre, those of Irish background (whether born in Ireland or in the UK) found such institutions more welcoming. Irish playwrights like Marina Carr and Irish immigrant playwrights like Anne Devlin or Ron Hutchinson, for instance, are able to work directly with West End theatres and with institutions like the Royal Court and the Royal Shakespeare Company (which commissions or accepts new plays as well as Shakespeare). Marie Jones's play *Stones in His Pockets* came from Belfast to the Tricycle Theatre in Kilburn (not a fringe venue, but not a West End or a landmark theater like the National), and then swiftly became a hit play and transferred to the West End. Female and male Irish-British playwrights like Shelagh Delaney (*A Taste of Honey*, Theatre Royal Stratford East, 1958) or Martin McDonagh (*The Cripple of Inishmaan*, National Theatre, 1997) have also gotten their work produced by building-based theatres and mainstream companies. In their account of women dramatists in Britain and Ireland, Trevor Griffiths and Margaret Llewellyn-Jones explain that their choice of 1958 as the starting date of their study was inspired by the production of *Taste*, which for them marked "a new way forward" for British drama.[27] This way forward was paved in large part by the numerous writers' initiatives and workshops launched in the 1970s and 1980s. Mary O'Malley was part of a writers' workshop led by the playwright Howard Brenton, through which her play *Once a Catholic* was commissioned by the theater in 1975, and the Royal Shakespeare Company produced her 1978 play *Look Out...Here Comes Trouble!* Decades later, Anne Devlin's *After Easter* was produced by the Royal Shakespeare Company in 1994.

Griffin goes on to draw striking parallels between the ways female characters have figured peripherally and have been defined largely through their relationships to male characters whose dilemmas drive the play's action, and the ways women playwrights and theater artists have been marginalized by theatre institutions and historiography. Much like postcolonial studies, feminist theatre historiography often works to expose and analyze untold, neglected, or misunderstood works and experiences, with an eye on the conditions that produce the oppression and silencing of women. Ten years prior to Griffin's book, Trevor Griffiths and Margaret Llewellyn Jones introduce their study of women playwrights by acknowledging the argument that devoting such studies "exclusively to women writers inevitably place their subject as the less privileged term in a binary opposition," but respond by remarking that "the fact remains that our ground has been defined for us negatively, by the vast majority of those who have studied British and Irish drama of the last thirty years, in the absence of women from their chapter headings, their indexes, and their studies."[28] Griffiths and Llewellyn-Jones do mention the significant contributions of scholars such as Sue-Ellen Case, Michelene Wandor, Helen Keyssar, Lesley Ferris, and Karen Malpede, but they argue that their wide-ranging studies "now need to be supplemented by more detailed and specific analyses such as ours which concentrate on geographically and historically limited periods."[29] One can take issue with their identification of the approach such analyses should take, but their survey of the critical field is nevertheless persuasive. Another project that emerged parallel to theirs in 1993 is Lizbeth Goodman's book *Contemporary Feminist Theatres: To Each Her Own*, which devotes one chapter to placing Black British theater companies such as Talawa, Theatre of Black Women, and Black Mime Theatre Women's Troop in an international context that includes North American, South African, and Caribbean companies and playwrights.

So how has the ground shifted since 1993? In the realm of theatre historiography, it has shifted tremendously, and at least in part in the direction of the analyses called for by Griffiths and Llewellyn-Jones. Between Griffiths and Llewellyn's and Griffin's books, many books and articles offered both revisionist histories of the roles of women on and off stage in the past decades (even centuries), as well as analyses and reviews of contemporary theatrical production and artists.[30]

With the assistance of Jane de Gay, Lizbeth Goodman published another book useful both for its documentation of a range of plays and companies and for its provision of interviews with women theater artists working in contemporary British and Irish theatre. Their "select" chronology of plays by women provides a snapshot of the range of works and artists from 1958 to 1996, suggesting both the breadth and the hidden depths of the stream in which the theater artists treated in this chapter have worked. For instance, playwrights of the 1950s and the 1960s such as Ann Jellicoe, Nell Dunn, and Shelagh Delaney centered their work on the lives and perspectives of female characters with their own dilemmas. In their focus on working-class characters and settings, these writers were highly successful but relatively less visible contributors to the largely male-dominated new wave of postwar British writing for the theatre championed by the Royal Court. Goodman's 1993 study of US and British feminist theatre (as distinguished from theatre made by and about women), works from "an overriding concern for the representation of the voices of the women who make feminist theatres," which she argues goes beyond but is indebted to the work of prior scholars on women's roles in the theatre.[31] Her work aims not strictly to engage in revisionist historiography that excavates women's presences and influences in theatre, but to provide what she describes as a larger critical frame for viewing and analyzing feminist theatre. In so doing, it contributes to a growing body of work dedicated to the examination of the conditions that not only shape such experiences and their representation, but also those that inform the production and reception of such creative work. Gabriele Griffin explains that *"Contemporary Black and Asian Women Playwrights in Britain* seeks to engage with a body of theatre work that has, on the whole, escaped critical attention" (9), work that should be considered an integral part of British theatre history. Griffin goes on to argue that even within this feminist historiography and aesthetic reconsideration:

> The invisibilization of that body of work in [feminist] theatre history replicates and reinforces the marginalization of Black and Asian women's work in British culture. This volume attempts to intervene in that process, arguing implicitly for the need to establish a critical and theoretical apparatus to accompany the publication of works by Black and Asian women playwrights in Britain.[32]

She notes that feminist theatre studies has paid more attention to these works than other fields, citing Mary Brewer's *Race, Sex, and Gender in Contemporary Women's Theatre* (1999) as the only work of its kind to emerge in Britain, though its emphasis falls more heavily on US playwrights. She goes on to examine where such work has been mentioned and finds the list limited, citing Goodman's work as well as that of Elaine Aston, May Joseph on Black British women playwrights (1998), Mary Karen Dahl on Black British playwrights both male and female in "Postcolonial British Theatre: Black Voices at the Center"

(1995), and Verma's contributions to *Theatre Matters* (Boon and Plastow, 1998) and *Contemporary British Theatre* (Shank, 1994). Since the publication of Griffin's book in 2003, more such work has emerged. As mentioned in the chapter opening, the work of this book owes much to the excavatory work and insights of scholars like Ann Fuchs and Geoffrey Davis, whose *Staging New Britain: Aspects of Black and South Asian Theatre Practice* contains groundbreaking essays by and about theatrical practices and artists who continue to profoundly influence British theater, such as Kully Thiarai, Yvonne Brewster, and Jatinder Verma, among others. Perhaps most exciting for those engaged in theater studies, the oral history and archival work of the *Unfinished Histories* project has resulted in the launching of a website and database of alternative theatre that provides researchers with access to a wealth of material on productions, companies, and artists.[33]

Conclusion

The cover of Yasmin Alibhai-Brown's *Imagining the New Britain* (2001) features a picture of Queen Elizabeth digitally altered to give her darker skin. Fast forward ten years to the cover of Aleks Sierz's *Rewriting the Nation: British Theatre Today* (2011), and the cover image is a young Black soccer fan with a flag of St. George painted on his face. Two visual icons of English, if not British, nationalism fused with the visual markers of "newness" for Britain. Both covers signal that what is "new" about Britain are the visible markers of a cultural hybridity, which returns us to the dueling narratives of British immigration history.

Alibhai-Brown's book contains the collected reflections of a thoughtful journalist on multiculturalism in Britain as she and others have defined it. A regular columnist for the *Independent* newspaper in London at the time of her book's publication, Alibhai-Brown has since become memoirist and performer of her own immigrant history in her stage play *Nowhere to Belong: Tales of An Extravagant Stranger*, which toured in 2008. Of Muslim Indian background, born and raised and university educated in Uganda, citizen and resident since the early 1970s in Britain, Alibhai-Brown is simultaneously critic, champion, and embodiment of the successes of British multiculturalism. While she invokes the arrival of the *Windrush* as a watershed moment for Britain, she characterizes it not as an originary moment for immigration, but instead as a signal of a transformation of the politics of postcolonial identity in Britain. Alibhai-Brown ironically refers to herself as part of the "last wave of the so-called immigration floods to sweep into this island," invoking the waves-and-floods-and-rivers-of-blood narrative discussed elsewhere in this book. She goes on to cite the work of Peter Fryer, Rozina Visram and other historians who counter this narrative with their accounts of the earliest immigrants to settle in Britain, noting for instance an African presence in Britain prior to the arrival of the Angles, from whom England derived its name.

The young man pictured on Sierz's book cover represents a similarly multivalent figure to the transformed Queen Elizabeth, one character in an ensemble of South Londoners in Roy Williams's pub-set *Sing Yer Heart Out for the Lads* (2002). Barry, an England fan with a "we're-all-mates" attitude towards the racism his friends alternately veil and flaunt, defines himself both through his "family" on the pub soccer team and against his actual father, whom he disparages as weak and hapless. He respects his brother Mark for serving his country as a soldier in Northern Ireland, while treating him dismissively for his supposed hypersensitivity to racism. The pub stands as a microcosm of contemporary Britain, containing myriad conflicts, tensions and alliances around its occupants' claims to respect, belonging, and ownership. Male entitlement surfaces in the claims of Gina's father Jimmy to authority in the pub, which belongs to her, as well as in the frequent sexual innuendoes and condescending remarks made to her by the pub regulars. Gina must navigate their sexism, the problems her teenage son Glenn denies or creates, and her personal and professional relationships with the pub regulars, all while trying to keep their racist remarks and her own prejudices in check. Alibhai-Brown's work ends with her "heartfelt" appeal to her fellow British citizens, in the wake of the Stephen Lawrence murder and inquiry into institutional racism in Britain, to bridge the divides created by persistent racism. Williams sets such divides within the volatile "home" in the St. George pub, and gives the play an ambiguous ending.

While the play offers an ambiguous and perhaps pessimistic vision of racial integration in Britain, the production itself offers a hopeful sign of the state of British theatres and their integration. Recent productions at the National Theatre have included the work of playwrights Tanika Gupta and Kwame Kwei-Armah, as well as Ayub Khan-Din's comedy *Rafta, Rafta* (2007) and Tara Arts' production of Hanif Kureishi's *The Black Album* (2009), though the former has been disparaged as inimical to the development of British Asian writing and of theatrical diversity, and the latter was not a commercial or critical success for the National.[1] Both the National and the Royal Court have expanded their offerings of international drama, including more works in translation.

Does this activity mean that British theater (and theaters) now represent homes for sustained participation and equal partnership between minority and majority theatre artists? Tara Arts Artistic Director Jatinder Verma and playwright Winsome Pinnock noted in the 1990s that much of the new writing and theatrical adaptations by Black British writers were relegated to studios, smaller stages and less experienced directors, an observation that may still hold true.[2] Resources have become more difficult to obtain and retain for all struggling theaters, which are often too consumed with the day-to-day business of managing their productions to dedicate any concerted effort to development and fundraising. Yet, leadership in building-based theater throughout England is overwhelmingly white, with only twelve Black British board members in all of England (four at the Tricycle in London, and four at the Theatre Royal Stratford East, and three at the Royal Court, leaving one board member in the rest of England).[3] It is understandable that immigrant and minority theater artists, finding themselves marginalized within the institutions and theatrical landscape of postwar Britain, would aspire to find the resources to establish a theatrical "home" or homes for their work. A building-based theater offers minority artists and audiences a stability and centrality and permanence often denied them through the discourses of nation, immigration, and race. Throughout the 1970s and 1980s, a building-based theatre for Black British theatre artists was proposed, discussed, and planned by multiple parties. It was ultimately abandoned, and is mentioned as a continuing need and aspiration in the most recent Arts Council report on the state of British theatre.[4]

A recent major Arts Council report on British theater, directly engages the question of ownership in its title, "Whose Theatre," while investigating the successes and failings of past theatrical initiatives and proposing strategies for the future, with the specific aim of promoting greater diversity and equality within theater, building in some ways on the work of the Eclipse Report on institutional racism in theater, which was published in 2001. That report's findings of a dearth of Black and Asian theatre professionals either on boards of theaters or active in their administration and other permanent staff triggered much discussion among cultural policymakers and theater artists about expanding participation in the making and marketing of theatre.

The "Sustained Theatre" project responds to those discussions and tries to assess any progress or setbacks in the time since the Eclipse Report's publication. "Whose Theatre" establishes a new term for the mainly Black and Asian artists, groups and institutions that constitute the key partners with the Arts Council on this initiative, referring to them as The Sector. A useful if somewhat *Battlestar Galactica* term, The Sector represents for the Arts Council a shift in emphasis from an identity-based approach to a focus on the "quality of the work," an unsettlingly ambiguous phrase.[5] When questioned about the need for a flagship venue or series of venues for The Sector, the participants had mixed responses, but the majority agreed on the value of establishing one or more mixed-use buildings owned and operated by members of The Sector. All agreed that development of the breadth, depth, and quality of theatrical work depended on training and other resources beyond physical space, and many argued that if existing spaces were more inclusive and welcoming of these artists, they might not feel the need for a dedicated venue. Concerns about segregation, draining of valuable resources in order to maintain such venues, and questions about the claims made on and about such spaces were met with affirmations that buildings offered a more secure foundation in the theatrical landscape.[6]

Interestingly, the Scottish National Theatre, which emerged in 2006 in the wake of devolution, declared the opposite aspiration and intention, seeking no building-based home, but rather a connection to multiple places and communities within Scotland. In their "manifesto," the company declares its intentions:

> The National Theatre of Scotland has no building; there has been no great capital project involving architects and contractors. Instead, we are taking theatre all over Scotland, working with the existing venues, touring and creating work within the theatre community. We have no bricks-and-mortar institutionalism to counter, nor the security of a permanent home in which to develop.[7]

It might be that the company's confidence in being a valued and equal partner in the making of culture in its community, and the absence of any recent history of calls for their displacement or "repatriation" allows them the freedom to dispense with a physical home for their theater.

Cultural theorist Homi Bhabha offers a potential strategy for such theatrical initiatives:

> What is theoretically innovative, and politically crucial, is the need to think beyond narratives of originary and initial subjectivities and to focus on those moments or processes that are produced in the articulation of cultural differences. These 'in-between' spaces provide the terrain for elaborating strategies of selfhood—singular or communal—that initiate new signs of identity, and innovative sites of collaboration and contestation in the act of defining the idea of society itself.[8]

Such examples do form inspiring responses to the challenge put forward by Jatinder Verma:

> The challenge of the coming millennium, in society as in theatre, is to embrace the Other: to learn how to become neighbours across divides of colour, language, and sensibility. If the theatrical enterprise is about the continual construction and reconstruction of a shared community—the dialogue between a given set of audiences and performers—then the question arises: how do we create the shared community with such diversity in our midst?

How then, does theater intervene in public life in constructive ways under these conditions? Taking individual theaters into consideration, one could make a case for the ways in which a Tricycle Theatre or a Theatre Royal Stratford

East have made an impact both upon their immediate borough or neighborhood (through youth theater initiatives, cheaper access to productions, public programs and events, participation in borough festivals and programs, and so on), and citywide through many of their productions. In some cases, such as *The Colour of Justice*, *Kat and the Kings*, *A Taste of Honey*, *Stones in His Pockets*, and *The Hostage* (the latter two being transfers to the London theaters), these theaters have launched productions that make a national and international impact, even sparking public debate and activism. Companies such as Tara Arts and Nitro (formerly Black Theatre Co-Operative) have fused Asian, African, Caribbean, and European theatrical and musical forms in their original productions and in adaptations of world classics. Along with these fusions, their productions mix music, physical theater, text and performance through collaborative processes that highlight theater's capacity for reinvention and transformation. The plays analyzed within this book, and the theaters that produce them do not necessarily meet the challenge set forth here. Some, indeed, reflect the seemingly insurmountable barriers to such creation of community or home both within theater and within society. These plays could at the very least *respond* to this challenge, self-consciously or otherwise, and in the process provide their own routes towards such shared community, and their own answers to Verma's aspiration for a truly shared ownership of British theater. Alibhai-Brown's appeal for more bridging of the divides in Britain echoes this aspiration. Both artists urge a fuller exploration of the shared fate and shared history that would lead to finding a welcoming home both on and off Britain's stages.

Notes

Introduction

1. Quentin Crisp, *The Naked Civil Servant* (London: Penguin Books, 1968).
2. Doreen Massey, *Space, Place, and Gender* (Minneapolis: University of Minnesota Press, 1994) 164.
3. Witold Rybszynski, *Home: A Short History of an Idea* (New York: Penguin Books, 1986).
4. MadanSarup, "Home and Identity," *Travellers Tales: Narratives of Home and Displacement* (London and New York: Rout ledge, 1994) 94.
5. Catherine Wiley and Fiona Barnes, editors, Introduction, *Homemaking: Women Writers and the Politics and Poetics of Home* (New York and London: Garland Publishing, 1996) xv.
6. Massey, 165.
7. Stuart Hall, "Reconstruction Work: Images of Postwar Black Settlement," in James Procter, ed. *Writing Black Britain 1948–1998* (Manchester and New York: Manchester University Press, 2000) 83.

Chapter One: Finding a Home on the Stage

1. Rajagopalan Radhakrishnan, *Diasporic Mediations: Between Home and Location* (Minneapolis: University of Minnesota Press, 1996)158.
2. Pearl Connor, "Our Olympian Struggle," (from the transcript of the opening address of 12th International Bookfair of Radical Black and Third World Books, given at the Camden Centre in London, England on March 23, 1995) 3.
3. Salman Rushdie, "Imaginary Homelands," in *Imaginary Homelands: Essays and Criticism 1981–1991* (London: Granta/Penguin Books, 1991) 10.
4. Homi Bhabha, *Nation and Narration* (London: Routledge, 1990) 1–2.
5. Bhabha, *Nation and Narration*, 2.
6. Rushdie, 12.
7. Massey, 145.
8. Wiley and Barnes, xvii.
9. Kathy Halbreich, "No Place (Like Home)" Exhibition Brochure, Walker Art Center, 9 March-8 June 1997, cover page.
10. Further reading: Paul Gilroy, *Between Camps: Nations, Cultures, and the Allure of Race* (London: Allen Lane, 2000).
11. Mary Karen Dahl, "Postcolonial British Theatre: Black Voices at the Center," in J. Ellen Gainor, ed., *Imperialism and Theatre* (London and New York: Routledge, 1995) 40–41.
12. James Procter, *Dwelling Places: Postwar Black British Writing* (Manchester and New York: Manchester University Press, 2003) 3.

Chapter Two: Narratives of Immigration and Theater in Postwar Britain

1. Poll cited in Lord's Report on Immigration (2008). http://www.publications. parliament.uk/pa/ld200708/ldselect/ldeconaf/82/82.pdf

2. Tony Judt, *Postwar: A History of Europe Since 1945* (New York: The Penguin Press, 2005) 280.

3. Judt, 299. See also Stephen Lacey, *British Social Realism: The New Wave in its Context* (London and New York: Routledge, 1995); and Samantha Lay, *British Social Realism: From Documentary to Brit Grit* (London: Wallflower Press, 2002).

4. Judt, 302.

5. Anthony Messina, "The Not So Silent Revolution: Postwar Migration to Western Europe", *World Politics*, 49.1 (1996) 130–154.

6. Susan J. Smith, "Immigration and nation-building in Canada and the United Kingdom," in Jan Penrose and Peter Jackson, editors, *Constructions of Race, Place and Nation* (Minneapolis: University of Minnesota Press, 1993) 54.

7. Judt, 331–332.

8. Smith, "Immigration and nation-building," 54.

9. Judt, 335–336.

10. Ian R. G. Spencer, *British Immigration Policy Since 1939: The Making of Multiracial Britain* (London: Routledge, 1997) Preface, xii.

11. Donley T. Studlar, "British Public Opinion, Colour Issues, and Enoch Powell: A Longitudinal Analysis," *British Journal of Political Science*, 4.3 (July 1974) 371–381.

12. A transcription of this speech can be found in Rex Collings, ed., *Reflections of a Statesman: The Writings and Speeches of Enoch Powell* (London: Bellew, 1991).

13. Robert Moore, and Tina Wallace, *Slamming the Door: The Administration of Immigration Control* (London: Martin Robertson and Company, 1975) 16–17.

14. Mary Hickman, "Reconstructing deconstructing 'race': British political discourse about the Irish in Britain", *Ethnic and Racial Studies*, 21.2 (March 1998) 290.

15. Hickman, "Reconstructing deconstructing 'race': British political discourse about the Irish in Britain," *Ethnic and Racial Studies*, 21.2 (March 1998) 288–307.

16. Paul Gilroy, *There Ain't No Black in the Union Jack* (Chicago: University of Chicago Press, 1991. First published in 1987) 46.

17. Panikos Panayi, *The Impact of Immigration: A Documentary History of the Effects and Experiences of Immigrants and Refugees in Britain Since 1945* (Manchester: Manchester University Press, 1999), 8–10.

18. See also: Panayi, *An Immigration History of Britain: Multicultural Racism Since c1800* (London: Longman, 2010); *Spicing Up Britain: The Multicultural History of British Food* (London: Reaktion, 2008); "Sausages, Waiters and Bakers: German Migrants and Culinary Transfer to Britain, c1850–1914," in Stefan Manz, Margrit Schulte Beerbühl and John R. Davis (Editors), *Migration and Transfer from Germany to Britain, 1660–1914* (Munich: Saur, 2007), pp. 149–61; and "The Immigrant Impact Upon London's Food Since c1850," in Peter J. Atkins, Peter Lummel and Derek Oddy (Editors), *Food and the City in Europe Since 1800* (Aldershot: Ashgate, 2007), 189–99.

19. Historians such as Tony Judt and PanosPanayi have described contemporary London and other cities in Britain as increasingly cosmopolitan, and point to postwar immigration as the critical factor in its transformation.

20. Such metaphors most famously appeared in the often-quoted remarks made by Enoch Powell (then an MP from Wolverhampton) and former Prime Minister Margaret Thatcher. A transcript of Powell's speech can be found in Rex Collings, ed., *Reflections of a Statesman: The Writings and Speeches of Enoch Powell* (London: Bellew, 1991). Thatcher's remarks were made in a television interview for which the full transcript is provided at the following URL: http://www.margaretthatcher.org/document/103485

21. Robert Winder, *Bloody Foreigners: The Story of Immigration to Britain* (London: Little, Brown, 2004) 336.

22. See for instance: Lydia Lindsey, "Halting the Tide: Responses to West Indian Immigration to Britain," *The Journal of Caribbean History*, 26.1 (1992) 62–95. This article breaks down the numbers of actual migrants and applications for passports from the Caribbean, and cites the push factors for emigration—such as a rate of 25% unemployment in Jamaica in 1946 (67). While she argues that it was less "real numbers" and more "imaginary fears" of British whites that drove racial tensions at this time, Lindsey often cites or echoes the rhetoric of the popular media, e.g. "tide," "exodus" without fully questioning it (62).

23. Ellis, David. "The Produce of More than One Country: Race, Identity, and Discourse in Post-Windrush Britain," *Journal of Narrative Theory*, 31.2 (Summer 2001) 216. See also: Peter Fryer, *Staying Power: The History of Black People in Britain*. London: Pluto Press, 1984.

24. The 1966 Census Report, as cited inDavid Dabydeen, John Gilmore and Cecily Jones, editors, *The Oxford Companion to Black British History* (Oxford: Oxford UP, 2008) 219.

25. "Island Lyrics," August 25, 2011. URL: http://www.islandlyrics.com/lyrics-lord_kitchener_lyrics-london_is_the_place_for_me_1960s.htm

26. *From War to Windrush*, Imperial War Museum, London (13 June 2008–1 November 2009). URL: http://www.iwm.org.uk/server/show/ConWebDoc.5290 Retrieved September 19, 2011.

27. An excellent analysis of this symbolic power can be found in an essay by Matthew Mead, "Empire Windrush: Cultural Memory and Archival Disturbance," *Moveable Type*, UCL English Online Journal, 3 (2007). Mead concludes that the "Windrush myth attains its symbolic resonance and power not through historical accuracy, but through the repeated inscription of this 'moment' on the national consciousness as a profound moment of cultural change that confirms, validates, and values the arrival and continuing presence of ethnically diverse communities" (121) but suggests elsewhere in the essay how such inscription serves multiple and contradictory agendas.

28. See, for instance: Susannah Clapp, "You're welcome to our country...," *The Observer*, February 15, 2009; Mark Espiner, "What to say about...England People Very Nice," *The Guardian*, February 13, 2009; Hussain Ismail, "Why the National Theatre's new play is racist and offensive," *The Guardian*, February 13, 2009; and Richard Bean, *England People Very Nice* (London: Oberon Books, 2009).

29. Winder, 10.

30. Daniel Defoe, "The True-Born Englishman. A Satyr," Project Gutenberg e-book prepared from *The Novels and Miscellaneous Works of Daniel De Foe, Volume 5* (London: Henry G. Bohn, 1855. First published in 1701.) Part I. Web.

31. Defoe, "The True-Born...," Part I. Web.

32. Robin Cook, in "Robin Cook's chicken tikka masala speech," extracted in *The Guardian*, April 19, 2001, 1–2. Web.

33. Clare Bayley, Preface to *The Container* (London: Nick Hern Books, 2007) 2.

34. See note 28.
35. Office of National Statistics, "Minority ethnic groups in the UK," (London: Crown Copyright 2002) 1.
36. Max Hebditch, in Nick Merriman, editor, *The Peopling of London* (London: The Museum of London, 1993) x.
37. Sukhdev Sandhu, *London Calling: How Black and Asian Writers Imagined a City* (London: Harper Perennial, 2005) xviii-xix.
38. Jacob Selway, "'English-Born Reputed Strangers': Birth and Descent in Seventeenth-Century London," *Journal of British Studies*, 44 (October 2005), 728.
39. On Tara Arts' tradaptations, see also Dominic Hingorani, *British Asian Theatre: Dramaturgy, Process, and Practice* (London: Palgrave MacMillan, 2010); Giovanna Buonanno, Victoria Sams, and Christiane Schlote, "Glocal Routes in British Asian Drama: Between Adaptation and Tradaptation," *Postcolonial Text*, 6:2 (2011) 1–18; and Victoria Sams, "Staging Visible Translations: Tradaptation in the work of Tara Arts Theatre Company," *ScrittureMigranti* (2008) 131–149.
40. Panayi, *The Impact of Immigration* (Manchester: Manchester UP, 1999) 2–3.
41. Sandhu, 12; Panayi, *Impact,* 3.
42. Sandhu, 13–14.
43. Colin Holmes, *John Bull's Island: Immigration and British Society 1851–1971* (Basingstoke and London: MacMillan Education, 1988) 20.
44. Panayi, *Impact,* 5–6.
45. Panayi, *Impact,* 5.
46. Sean Hutton, "The Irish in London," in *The Peopling of London,* 118.
47. Colin Holmes, *John Bull's Island: Immigration and British Society 1851–1971*. Basingstoke and London: MacMillan Education, 1988) 39.
48. Hutton, in *The Peopling of London,* 119.
49. Visram, in *The Peopling of London,* 171.
50. David Dabydeen, John Gilmore and Cecily Jones, editors, *The Oxford Companion to Black British History* (Oxford: Oxford UP, 2008) 544.
51. Dilip Hiro. "The Coolies of Empire," in *Black British, White British* (New York and London: Monthly Review Press, 1971) 99–109.
52. Hiro, *Black British, White British,* 103.
53. Visram, 172.
54. Hiro, 103.
55. Hiro, 104.
56. Hiro, 106.
57. Hiro, 106.
58. OPCS (1993) 1991 Census, and Ethnic group country of birth, Great Britain Vol. 1. Table 5.
59. Visram, 171.
60. Visram, 172, and program introduction for *Balti Kings...*
61. Amit Roy. "Why there is no business like Curry business," from the programme for *Balti Kings* (2000). Courtesy of Tamasha Theatre Company.
62. Amit Roy. "Why there is no business like Curry business," from the programme for *Balti Kings* (2000). Courtesy of Tamasha Theatre Company.
63. Graham Ley, "Theatre of Migration and the search for a multicultural aesthetic: Twenty years of Tara Arts," in New Theatre Quarterly (Cambridge: Cambridge University Press), V. 13, n. 52, 349.

64. Kausalya Santhanam, "Transcending Alienness," The Hindu (Online Edition), 17 March 2002, Sunday Magazine section.

65. Jatinder Verma, "'Braids' and Theatre Practice". Transcript of a talk given at the British Braids Conference at Brunel University, Twickenham Campus, on 20 April 2001 (pages not numbered, p.4 by my count)

66. Jatinder Verma, "Asian Arts in the 21st Century," speech given at Waterman Arts Centre, March 24, 2003. Courtesy of Tara Arts Archive (June 28, 2005).

67. Verma, "Are We Visible?" talk given at Peshkar Conference, Oldham, November 13, 2001. From the Tara Arts Archive.

68. Paul Gilroy, *There Ain't No Black in the Union Jack* (Chicago: University of Chicago Press, 1991. Originally published in 1987) 45.

69. Peter Osborne, "Behind Enoch Powell's monstrous image lay a man of exceptional integrity." *The Telegraph*, 13 June 2012.

70. Gilroy, 45–46.

71. Gilroy, 46.

72. Gilroy, 48.

73. Kathleen Paul, *Whitewashing Britain* (Ithaca, NY: Cornell University Press, 1997) 105.

74. Tom Murphy, *A Whistle in the Dark*, in *Plays: Four* (London: Methuen Drama, 1989) 10.

75. Paul, *Whitewashing Britain*, 107.

76. Mary Hickman, "Reconstructing deconstructing 'race': British political discourses about the Irish in Britain," *Ethnic and Racial Studies*, 21:2, 303.

77. Hickman, "Reconstructing deconstructing…," 305.

78. Mary J. Hickman and Bronwen Walter, *Discrimination and the Irish Community in Britain: A Report of Research Undertaken for the Commission for Racial Equality* (London: CRE, 1997).

79. Mary Hickman, "Reconstructing deconstructing 'race': British political discourses about the Irish in Britain", *Ethnic and Racial Studies*, 21: 2, 304.

80. Mary J. Hickman and Bronwen Walter, *Discrimination and the Irish Community in Britain: A Report of Research Undertaken for the Commission for Racial Equality* (London: CRE, 1997).

81. Colin Chambers provides a well-detailed account of the activism of these organizations, and the opportunities for collaboration that they generated. The work of Indian-Irish actor Aubrey Menon and African-American actor and singer Paul Robeson is particularly notable. Chambers, *Black and Asian Theatre in Britain* (London and New York: Routledge, 2011). See Chapters 4 and 5 in particular.

82. Jeremy Poynting, "Publishing in the Cracks," *Small Axe Salon,* Issue 5 (June 2011), web.

83. Susheila Nasta, "Setting up Home in a City of Words: Sam Selvon's London novels," *Other Britain, Other British,* 48.

84. Chambers, 105–123.

85. Sandhu, *London Calling*, xxiii.

86. Stone, Judy. *Studies in West Indian Literature: Theatre* (London: Macmillan Caribbean, 1994) 168.

87. Roland Rees, *Fringe First: Pioneers of Fringe Theatre on Record* (London: Oberon Books, 1992) 96–97; and Victoria Sams, interview with Mustapha Matura, November 19, 1999.

88. Chambers, 143.

89. Chambers, 147.

90. Chambers, 147.

91. Chambers, 148.

92. Chambers, 148.

93. Chambers 150.

94. "What's in a name?" Talawa Company Profile (provided by company's administrative assistant on 10 November 1999).

95. "Talawa's mission statement," in Talawa Company profile.

96. Naseem Khan, *The Arts Britain Ignores* (London: Arts Council Report, 1976).

97. Barnaby King, "Landscapes of Fact and Fiction: Asian Theatre Arts in Britain", in *New Theatre Quarterly* (Cambridge: Cambridge University Press), V. 16, n.1, February 2000) 27–28.

98. Sarah Dadswell and Graham Ley, editors, *British South Asian Theatres: A Documented History* (Exeter: University of Exeter Press, 2011) 1, 3.

99. Dadswell and Ley, 3.

100. Jatinder Verma, "'Binglishing' the Stage: a generation of Asian Theatre in England," in Richard Boon and Jane Plastow, eds.,*Theatre Matters: performance and culture on the world stage* (Cambridge: Cambridge University Press, 1998) 127.

101. For further accounts of the work of these and more British South Asian organizations and artists, see Dadswell and Ley, *British South Asian Theatres: A Documented History.* See also the companion DVD, which contains images and performance clips.

102. "Eclipse Report: Developing Strategies to Combat Racism in Theatre," conference transcript, Nottingham Playhouse, 12v13 June 2001. Published by Arts Council of England in 2002.

103. Eamonn Hughes, "'Lancelot's Position': The Fiction of Irish Britain," *Other Britain, Other British*, 142.

104. Hughes, 142.

105. Yasmin Alibhai, "Where it is eminently desirable to be young, gifted, and Asian," *The Guardian*, 8 May 1986.

106. For further information, see: Theatre Museum: http://www.vam.ac.uk/content/articles/b/black-and-asian-performance-a-users-guide/ SALIDAA: http://salidaa.com/salidaa/site/Home; Irish Theatrical Diaspora Project: http://www. irishtheatricaldiaspora.net/about.html; British Asian Theatre Archive: http://spa.exeter.ac.uk/drama/research/britishasian/welcome.shtml; and Nasta: http://www.open.ac.uk/Arts/south-asians-making-britain/index.shtml.

Chapter Three: Journeys and Arrivals

1. Marie Jones, *Four Plays by Charabanc Theatre Company: Reinventing Woman's Work* (Oxford: Oxford University Press, 2007).

2. For further reading: Yasmin Alibhai-Brown, *The Settler's Cookbook: A Memoir of Love, Migration and Food* (London: Portobello Books, 2008); Mike Phillips, *London Crossings: A Biography of Black Britain* (London and New York: Continuum, 2001); Onyekachi Wambu, editor, *Hurricane Hits England: An Anthology of Writing About Black Britain* (London and New York: Continuum, 2000); James Procter, editor, *Writing Black Britain: 1948–1998* (Manchester: Manchester UP, 2000).

3. Mustapha Matura, "Nice," in *As Time Goes By and Black Pieces* (London: Calder and Boyars, 1972) 69, 81.

4. Edgar White, *The Nine Night* (London: Methuen Drama, 1984) 12.

5. White, *The Nine Night*, 13.

6. White, *The Nine Night*, 13.

7. "From War to *Windrush*," Imperial War Museum, June 2008–March 2009 (Exhibition). "Moving Here: 200 Years of Migration to England." Website and series of exhibitions directed by National Archives. <http://www.movinghere.org.uk>

8. Anne Devlin, *After Easter* (London: Faber and Faber, 1994) 13.

9. Phillips, Caryl, *Where There Is Darkness* (Ambergate: Amber Lane Press, 1982) 20.

10. For further reading on colonial science, see: Sander L. Gilman, *Difference and Pathology: Stereotypes of Sexuality, Race, and Madness* (Ithaca: Cornell Univ. Press, 1985) and Nancy Stepan, *The Idea of Race in Science: Great Britain, 1800–1960* (London: Macmillan, 1982).

11. Wole Soyinka, "Telephone Call", in Onyekachi Wambu, editor, *Hurricane Hits England: An Anthology of Writing About Black Britain* (London and New York: Continuum, 2000). Poem first read at the Royal Court Theatre in 1959.

12. Devlin, *After Easter,* 9.

13. Delaney, Enda. *The Irish in Post-war Britain* (Oxford: Oxford UP, 2007) 62.

14. Bains, Harwant, *Blood* (London: Oberon, 1989) 8.

15. Michael Abbensetts, *Sweet Talk* (London: Methuen, 1974) 12.

16. Matura, Mustapha. *Plays: One* (London: Methuen, 1991) 14.

17. Matura, *As Time Goes By,* 62.

18. Ayub Khan-Din, *Rafta, Rafta* (London: Nick Hern Books, 2007) 26.

19. Ayub Khan-Din, *Rafta, Rafta,* 27.

20. Kwame Kwei-Armah, *Elmina's Kitchen*, in *Plays: 1* (London: Methuen Drama, 2009) 90.

21. Jim McCarthy, "Missing You," recorded by Christy Moore on *Live at the Point* (Dublin: Grapevine Records, 1994).

22. Stuart Hall, "Calypso Kings," *The Guardian,* 28 June 2002. URL: http://www.guardian.co.uk/culture/2002/jun/28/nottinghillcarnival2002.nottinghillcarnival

23. Jimmy Murphy, *The Kings of the Kilburn High Road* (London: Oberon Books, 2000) 18.

24. Murphy, 47.

25. Delaney, Enda. *The Irish in Post-war Britain* (Oxford: Oxford UP, 2007).

Chapter Four: Patriarchy in Crisis

1. Homi Bhabha, "The World and the Home," in Anne McClintock, Aamir Mufti, and Ella Shohat, editors, *Dangerous Liaisons: Gender, Nation, and Postcolonial Perspectives* (Minneapolis and London: University of Minnesota Press, 1997) 445.

2. Edward Said, "The Art of Displacement: Mona Hatoum's Logic of Irreconcilables," in *The Entire World as a Foreign Land* (London: Tate Gallery Publishing, Ltd., 2000) 15.

3. Nicholas Grene, *The Politics of Irish Drama: Plays in Context from Boucicault to Friel* (Cambridge: Cambridge University Press, 1999) 197.

4. Grene, *The Politics of Irish Drama,* 197.

5. Stephen Lacey. *British Realist Theatre: The New Wave in its Context 1956–1965* (London and New York: Routledge, 1995) 29.

6. Lacey, 16.

7. Fintan O'Toole, *Tom Murphy: The Politics of Magic* (Dublin: New Island Books, 1994), 29.

8. O'Toole, *Politics of Magic,* 58.

9. O'Toole, *Politics of Magic,* 58.

10. Richard Kearney. *Transitions: Narratives in Modern Irish Culture* (Dublin: Wolfhound Press, 1988) 150–161.

11. O'Toole, *Politics of Magic,* 36–37.

12. O'Toole, *Politics of Magic*, 67–68.
13. O'Toole, *Politics of Magic*, 67–68.
14. Tom Murphy. *A Whistle in the Dark*, in *Plays: 4* (London: Methuen Drama, 1989) 13.
15. Murphy, *Whistle* 13.
16. O'Toole, *Politics of Magic*, 53.
17. O'Toole, *Politics of Magic*, 54.
18. Kearney, *Transitions*, 162–163.
19. O'Toole, *Politics of Magic*, 12.
20. Review in *Evening Herald*, as quoted in O'Toole, *Politics of Magic*, 12.
21. O'Toole links Michael Carney to Stephen Dedalus and Christy Mahon, among other celebrated fictional rebellious sons, arguing for parallel readings of these works' comic critiques of the false heroics and provincialism of those who mythologize their past. He writes: "After four decades of the new Ireland that Joyce and Synge looked forward to, *A Whistle in the Dark* shows a similar struggle between a young man and his father, a similar revolt against a man who is a praiser of his own past [citing Declan Kiberd's expression], who is, like Synge's peasants dependent on a false notion of heroism to stem the pain of failure. But this time the father is not so easy to kill, and the outcome is tragic rather than comic. This is what makes it a post-nationalist play." *Politics of Magic*, 69.
22. Kenneth Tynan, "Wolves at the Door," *Observer*, September 17, 1961.
23. Tynan, "Wolves at the Door".
24. Grene, *The Politics of Irish Drama*, 196.
25. Michael Billington, "East Is Best," *Guardian*, 25 November 1996, p. 8; Charles Spencer, "Rich Mix of Culture and Comedy," *Daily Telegraph*, 25 November 1996; and John Peter, "Crossed Countries," *Sunday Times*, 1 December 1996.
26. Tynan, "Wolves at the Door".
27. Charles Spencer, "Painful but True," *Daily Telegraph*, July 12, 1989.
28. Khan-Din, Introduction, *East is East* (London: Nick Hern Books, 1999) ix-x.
29. Khan-Din (1997) 30.
30. Khan-Din (1997) 65.
31. Khan-Din (1997) 36.

Chapter Five: Different for Girls

1. See: Susan Croft, "Black Women Playwrights in Britain," in Trevor Griffiths and Margaret Llewellyn-Jones, editors, *British and Irish Women Dramatists Since 1958* (Bristol, PA and Buckingham: Open University Press, 1993) 84–98; Ann Fuchs and Geoffrey V. Davis, editors, *Staging New Britain: Aspects of Black and South Asian British Theatre Practice* (Oxford: Peter Lang, 2006).
2. May Rosalind Joseph, *Nomadic Identities: The Performance of Citizenship* (Minneapolis: University of Minnesota Press, 1999) 117.
3. Gabriele Griffin, "Theatres of Difference: The Politics of 'Redistribution' and 'Recognition' in the Plays of Contemporary Black and Asian Women Playwrights in Britain," *Feminist Review*, No. 84, Postcolonial Theatres Issue (2006) 12.
4. Gabriele Griffin, *Contemporary Black and Asian Women Playwrights in Britain* (Cambridge: Cambridge University Press, 2003) 25.

5. Gabriele Griffin, "Theatres of Difference: The Politics of 'Redistribution' and 'Recognition' in the Plays of Contemporary Black and Asian Women Playwrights in Britain", *Feminist Review*, No. 84, Postcolonial Theatres Issue (2006) 16.

6. Gurpreet Kaur Bhatti, *Behzti (Dishonour)* (London: Oberon Books, 2005).

7. Michael Coveney, "Stage Scandal Revisited: Gurpreet Kaur Bhatti's New Play," *The Independent*, 27 March 2010. Opening night was December 18, 2004. The production closed two days later.

8. Margaret Llewellyn-Jones, "Claiming a Space: 1969–1978," in *British and Irish Women Dramatists Since 1958* (Bristol, PA and Buckingham: Open University Press, 1993) 31–32.

9. Yasmin Alibhai-Brown, "Welcome Home", in Linda Brogan and Polly Teale, *Speechless* (London: Nick Hern, 2011).

10. Enrica Cerquoni, *"Ourselves Alone, Heartlanders, After Easter,"* in *The Methuen Guide to Contemporary Irish Playwrights* (London; Methuen Drama, 2010) 62.

11. Cerquoni, *"Ourselves…,"* 66.

12. Griffin, *Black and Asian Women Playwrights*, 19.

13. Patricia Schroeder, *The Feminist Possibilities of Dramatic Realism* (Madison, NJ: Farleigh Dickinson University Press, 1996) 150.

14. Gabriele Griffin, "Theatres of Difference: The Politics of 'Redistribution' and 'Recognition' in the Plays of Contemporary Black and Asian Women Playwrights in Britain," *Feminist Review*, No. 84, Postcolonial Theatres Issue (2006), 11.

15. Pearl Connor-Mogotsi, "Our Olympian Struggle: The opening address of the 12th International Bookfair of Radical Black and Third World Books," The Camden Centre London, 23 March 1995. Speech transcript, 1.

16. Paraphrased from Pearl Connor, "BlackGrounds: Pearl Connor," June 25, 1997. One of a series of video interviews jointly produced by Talawa Theatre Company and the Theatre Museum. From the Theatre Museum Archive (now housed at the V&A Museum/Olympia).

17. Alaknanda Samarth, "BlackGrounds: Alaknanda Samarth," May 19,1997. One of a series of video interviews jointly produced by Talawa Theatre Company and the Theatre Museum. From the Theatre Museum Archive (now housed at the V&A Museum/ Olympia).

18. Yvonne Brewster, *The Undertaker's Daughter* (London: BlackAmber Books, 2004) 45–46.

19. Lizbeth Goodman, *Contemporary Feminist Theatres: To Each Her Own* (London and New York: Routledge, 1993) 6.

20. Lizbeth Goodman and Jane de Gay, *Feminist Stages: Interviews with Women in Contemporary British Theatre* (Amsterdam: Harwood Academic Publishers, 1996) 123–125.

21. BBC interview with Yvonne Brewster. Web. www.bbc.co.uk/programmes/ p00x0130

22. Brewster, as interviewed in Goodman and de Gay, *Feminist Stages*, 123.

23. Brewster, as interviewed in Goodman and de Gay, *Feminist Stages*, 126.

24. Lizbeth Goodman, *Contemporary Feminist Theatres: To Each Her Own* (London and New York: Routledge, 1993) 149.

25. "About Kali", Kali Theatre Company website. http://www.kalitheatre.co.uk/ about/about.html Retrieved September 27, 2011.

26. "Writer Support," Kali Theatre Company website. http://www.kalitheatre.co.uk/writer-support/writer-support.html Retrieved September 30, 2011.

27. Trevor Griffiths and Margaret Llewellyn-Jones, editors, *British and Irish Women Dramatists Since 1958: A Critical Handbook* (Buckingham and Philadelphia: Open University Press, 1993) 4.

28. Griffiths and Jones, editors, *British and Irish Women Dramatists Since 1958*, 1.

29. Griffiths and Jones, editors, *British and Irish...*, 3.
30. For example, the work of Elaine Aston, Janelle Reinelt and others.
31. Lizbeth Goodman, *Contemporary Feminist Theatres,* 6.
32. Gabrielle Griffin, *Contemporary Black and Asian Female Playwrights in Britain* (Cambridge: Cambridge University Press, 2003) 35.
33. Susan Croft, Director, *Unfinished Histories* (website). <http://www. unfinishedhistories.com>

Conclusion

1. Bancil, Parv. "Where are our modern British Asian plays?", *The Guardian* http://www.guardian.co.uk/stage/theatreblog/2008/nov/26/british-asian-theatre
2. Mentioned in personal interview with Jatinder Verma, December 6, 1999. Echoed by Winsome Pinnock in Vera Gottlieb and Colin Chambers, editors, *Theatre in a Cool Climate* (Oxford: Amber Lane Press, 1999) p. 36.
3. Michael Billington, "White Out", *The Guardian,* October 18, 2000.
4. http://www.sustainedtheatre.org.uk/about
5. "Whose Theatre: The Sustained Theatre Consultation" (report of a study conducted by Arts Council England, 2005) 13.
6. "Whose Theatre: The Sustained Theatre Consultation" (report of a study conducted by Arts Council England, 2005).
7. "Manifesto," on the National Theatre of Scotland website: www. nationaltheatrescotland. com/content/default.asp?page=s7_7 Retrieved October 5, 2011.
8. Homi Bhabha, *The Location of Culture* (New York: Routledge, 1994) 1–2.

Bibliography

Primary Sources

Abbensetts, Michael. *Sweet Talk*. London: Methuen Drama, 1973.

———. *Samba*. London: Methuen Drama, 1980.

Addai, Levi David.*House of Agnes*. London: Methuen Drama, 2008.

Agboluaje, Oladipo. *The Hounding of David Oluwale*. London: Oberon Modern Plays, 2009.

Alawi, Karim. *A Colder Climate*. London: Methuen Drama, 1986.

Anand, Mulk Raj. *Across the Black Waters*. Delhi: Orient Paperbacks, 2008. First published in 1939.

Bains, Harwant. *Blood*. London: Methuen Drama, 1989.

Bancil, Parv. *Crazyhorse*. London: Faber Playscripts, 1997.

Bayley, Claire. *The Container*. London: Nick Hern Books, 2007.

Bhatti, Gurpreet Kaur. *Behzti (Dishonour)*. London: Oberon Books, 2004.

Bean, Richard. *England People Very Nice*. London: Oberon Books, 2009.

Brenton, Howard, and Tunde Ikoli. *Sleeping Policemen*. London: Methuen, 1984.

Brogan, Linda and Polly Teale, *Speechless*. London: Nick Hern Books, 2011.

Carter, Ruth. *A Yearning*. London: Nick Hern Books/Tamasha Plays, 1999.

D'Aguiar, Fred. *A Jamaican Airman Foresees his Death*, in Yvonne Brewster, editor, *Black Plays Three*. London: Methuen Drama, 1989.

Delaney, Shelagh. *A Taste of Honey*. London: Theatre Workshop, 1956.

Devlin, Anne. *After Easter*. London: Faber and Faber, 1994.

Fagon, Alfred. *Plays*. London: Oberon Books, 1999. *Lonely Cowboy* first published in Yvonne Brewster, editor, *Black Plays* in 1987 by Methuen London Ltd. *11 Josephine House* first produced in 1972 at Almost Free Theatre. *The Death of a Black Man* first produced in 1975 at Hampstead Theatre.

George, Kadija. *Six Plays by Black and Asian Women Writers*. London: Aurora Metro Press, 1993.

Gupta, Tanika. *Gladiator Games*. London: Oberon Books, 2005.

———. *Fragile Land*. London: Oberon Modern Plays, 2003.

Hutchinson, Ron. *Rat in the Skull*. London: Methuen Drama, 1984.

Ikoli, Tunde. *Scrape off the Black*. London: Oberon Books, 1998. First published in Yvonne Brewster, editor, *Black Plays Three*. London: Methuen Drama, 1989.

Keane, John B. *Many Young Men of Twenty; Moll; The Chastitute*. Cork: Mercier Press, 1991.

Khan-Din, Ayub. *Rafta, Rafta*. London: Nick Hern Books, 2007.

———. *East Is East*. London: Nick Hern Books, 1997.

Kureishi, Hanif. *The Black Album*. London: Faber and Faber, 2009.

———. *My Beautiful Laundrette and Other Writings*. London: Faber and Faber, 1996.

———. *Outskirts and Other Plays*. London: Faber and Faber, 1992.

Kwei-Armah, Kwame. *Elmina's Kitchen*. London: Methuen Drama, 2003.

Matura, Mustapha. *Six Plays*. London: Methuen Drama, 1992.

Moffat, Nigel. *Mama Decemba*. London: Faber and Faber, 1987.

Murphy, Darren. *Irish Blood, English Heart.* London: Oberon Modern Plays, 2011.

Murphy, Jimmy. *Two Plays: The Kings of the Kilburn High Road; Brothers of the Brush.* London: Oberon Books, 2001.

Murphy, Tom. *Plays: 4.* London: Methuen Press, 1989. Introduction by Fintan O'Toole.

O'Malley, Mary. *Once a Catholic.* London: Samuel French, Inc., 1978.

———. *Look Out...Here Comes Trouble!* Ambergate: Amber Lane Press, 1979.

Norton-Taylor, Richard. *The Colour of Justice.* London: Oberon Books, 1999.

Phillips, Caryl. *Playing Away.* London: Faber and Faber, 1987.

———. *Strange Fruit.* Ambergate: Amber Lane Press, 1981.

———. *Where There Is Darkness.* Ambergate: Amber Lane Press, 1982.

Pinnock, Winsome. *Leavetaking.* In Kate Harwood, editor, *First Run: New Plays By New Writers.* London: Nick Hern Books, 1989.

———. *Mules.* London: Faber and Faber, 1996.

———. *The Rebirth of Robert Samuels.* London: Faber and Faber, 1995.

———. *Talking in Tongues.* In Yvonne Brewster, editor, *Black Plays Three.* London: Methuen Drama, 1989.

River, Sol. B. *48–98.* In Sol B. River, *Plays Two.* London: Oberon Books, 2003.

Selvon, Samuel. *Lonely Londoners.* London: Allen Wingate Publishers, 1956.

———. *Moses Ascending.* Oxford: Heinemann, 1984. Originally published in 1975.

———. *Moses Migrating.* Washington, D.C.: Three Continents, 1992. Originally published in 1983.

Stivicic, Tena. *Fragile!* London: Nick Hern Books, 2007.

Walsh, Enda. *The Walworth Farce.* London: Nick Hern Books, 2007.

Wesker, Arnold. *The Kitchen.* In *Volume 2: The Kitchen and Other Plays.* London: Penguin Books, 1976. *The Kitchen* first published by Penguin Books in 1960.

White, Edgar. *Lament for Rastafari (3 Plays).* London and New York: Marion Boyars, Ltd., 1983.

———. *Redemption Song (3 Plays).* London and New York: Marion Boyars, Ltd., 1985.

———. *The Nine Night and Ritual By Water.* London: Methuen, 1984.

Williams, Roy. *Sucker Punch.* London: Methuen Drama, 2010.

———. *Sing Yer Heart Out for the Lads.* London: Methuen, 2002.

Secondary Sources

Akenson, Donald Harman. *The Irish Diaspora: A Primer.* Belfast: The Institute of Irish Studies/Queen's University of Belfast, 1993.

Alibhai-Brown, Yasmin. *Imagining the New Britain.* London: Routledge, 2001.

———. *Some of My Best Friends Are... Collected Writings 1989–2004.* London: Politico's, 2004.

Anderson, Benedict. *Imagined Communities: Reflections on the Origin and Spread of Nationalism.* London: Verso, 1983.

Anderson, Doug. "Bums on Seats: Parties, Art, and Politics in London's East End." *The Drama Review,* 35.1 (Spring 1991): 43.

Anderson, Malcolm, and Eberhard Bort, eds. *The Irish Border: History, Politics, Culture.* Liverpool: Liverpool University Press, 1999.

Anderson, Michael, editor. *British Population History.* Cambridge: Cambridge University Press, 1996.

Ansorge, Peter. *From Liverpool to Los Angeles.* London: Faber and Faber, 1995.

———. *Disrupting the Spectacle: Five Years of Experimental and Fringe Theatre in Britain.* London: Pitman, 1975.

Appadurai, Arjun. *Modernity at Large: Cultural Dimensions of Globalization*. Minneapolis and London: University of Minnesota Press, 1996.

Banham, Martin, Errol Hill, and George Woodyard, editors. *The Cambridge Guide to African and Caribbean Theatre*. Cambridge: Cambridge University Press, 1994.

Benson, Eugene, and L.W. Connolly, editors. *Encyclopedia of Post-Colonial Literatures in English*. London: Routledge, 1994.

Bhabha, Homi. *The Location of Culture*. London and New York: Routledge, 1994.

———. "The World and the Home." In Anne McClintock, Aamir Mufti, and Ella Shohat, editors, *Dangerous Liaisons: Gender, Nation, and Postcolonial Perspectives*. Minneapolis and London: University of Minnesota Press, 1997.

———. *Nation and Narration*. London: Routledge, 1990.

Bharucha, Rustom. *The Politics of Cultural Practice: Thinking Through Theatre in an Age of Globalization*. Hanover and London: Wesleyan University Press/University Press of New England, 2000.

Bhat, Ashok, Roy Carr Hill, and Sushel Ohn, editors. *Britain's Black Population*. London: Gower Publishing, 1982.

Billington, Michael. *State of the Nation: British Theatre Since 1945*. London: Faber and Faber, 2007.

Boon, Richard, and Jane Plastow, editors. *Theatre Matters: Performance and Culture on the World Stage*. Cambridge: Cambridge University Press, 1998.

Bose, Sugata, and Ayesha Jalal. *Modern South Asia: History, Culture, Political Economy*. London and New York: Routledge, 1997.

Bourne, Stephen. *Black in the British Frame: The Black Experience in British Film and Television*. New York: Continuum, 2001.

Boyce, D. George. *Nationalism in Ireland*. London: Routledge, 1982.

Bracewell, Michael. *England Is Mine*. London: Harper Collins, 1997.

Bradwell, Mike, editor. *The Bush Theatre Book: Twenty-Five Years*. London: Methuen Drama, 1997.

Brah, Avtar. *Cartographies of Diaspora: Contesting Identities*. London and New York: Routledge, 1996.

Braziel, Jana Evans, and Anita Mannur. *Theorizing Diaspora*. Oxford: Blackwell, 2003.

Brennan, Tim. "Writing from Black Britain." *Literary Review*, 34.1 (Fall 1990) 5.

Brenton, Howard. *Hot Irons: Diaries, Essays, Journalism*. London: Methuen, 1995.

Bygott, David. *Black and British*. London: Oxford University Press, 1992.

Casey, Edward. *Getting Back into Place*. Bloomington, Indiana: Indiana UP, 1993.

———. *Remembering*. Bloomington, Indiana: Indiana UP, 1987.

Chambers, Colin. *Black and Asian Theatre in Britain: A History*. London and New York: Routledge, 2011.

Chambers, Colin, and Vera Gottlieb, editors. *Theatre in a Cool Climate*. Oxford: Amber Lane Press, 1999.

Chambers, Ian, and Lidia Curti, editors. *The Post-Colonial Question: Common Skies, Divided Horizons*. London and New York: Routledge, 1996.

Clifford, James. *Routes: Travel and Translation in the Late Twentieth Century*. Cambridge: Harvard University Press, 1997.

Cohen, Philip, and Harwant S. Bains, editors. *Multi-Racist Britain*. London: MacMillan Education, 1988.

Cohen, Robin, and Zig Layton-Henry, editors. *Politics and Migration*. Cheltenham: Edward Elgar, 1988.

Collings, Rex, editor. *Reflections of a Statesman: The Writings and Speeches of Enoch Powell*. London: Bellew, 1991.

Crow, Brian, and Chris Banfield. *An Introduction to Postcolonial Theatre*. Cambridge: Cambridge University Press, 1996.

Dabydeen, David, John Gilmore, and Cecily Jones, editors. *The Oxford Companion to Black British History*. Oxford: Oxford UP, 2007.

Davis, Geoffrey, and Ann Fuchs, editors. *Staging New Britain: Aspects of Black and South Asian Theatre Practice*. Brussels: Peter Lang, 2006.

Day-Lewis, Sean. *Talk of Drama: Views of the Television Dramatist Now and Then*. Luton: University of Luton Press, 1998.

Delaney, Enda. *The Irish in Post-War Britain*. Oxford: Oxford University Press, 2007.

Devine, Harriet. *Looking Back: Playwrights at the Royal Court.*Lonodn: Faber and Faber, 2006.

Diamond, Elin. *Performance and Cultural Politics*. London and New York: Routledge, 1996.

Dromgoole, Dominic. *The Full Room: An A-Z of Contemporary Playwriting*. London: Methuen, 2000.

Duncan, James, and David Ley, editors. *Place, Culture, Representation*. London and New York: Routledge, 1993.

Edgar, David, editor. *State of Play: Playwrights on Playwriting*. London: Faber and Faber, 1999.

Ellis, David. "The Produce of More Than One Country: Race, Identity, and Discourse in Post-Windrush Britain." *Journal of Narrative Theory*, 31.2 (Summer 2001).

Ellis, Peter Berresford. *A History of the Irish Working Class*. London: Pluto Press, 1985. First published in 1972 by Victor Gollancz Limited.

Ethnicity in the 1991 Census: Volume One—Demographic Characteristics of the Ethnic Minority Populations. London: Office of Population Censuses and Surveys, 1996.

Featherstone, M., editor. *Global Culture*. London: Sage Press, 1990.

Finer, Catherine Jones, editor. *Migration, Immigration, and Social Policy*. London: John Wiley, 2006.

Fryer, Peter. *Staying Power: The History of Black People in Britain*. London: Pluto Press, 1984.

Fusco, Coco. *English Is Broken Here: Notes on Cultural Fusion in the Americas*. New York: New Press, 1997.

Gainor, J. Ellen, editor. *Imperialism and Theatre*. London and New York: Routledge, 1996.

Gardner, Lyn. "Who's Asian Theatre For? Asian Communities or Everybody?" *Guardian*, 29 January 1997.

Genet, Jacqueline, and Elisabeth Hellegouarc'h, editors. *Actes de Colloques de Caeen: Studies on the Contemporary Irish Theatre*. Caen: Université de Caen, 1991.

Gikandi, Simon. *Maps of Englishness: Writing Identity in the Culture of Colonialism*. New York: Columbia University Press, 1996.

Gilbert, Helen, and Joanne Tompkins. *Post-Colonial Drama: Theory, Practice, Politics*. London: Routledge, 1996.

Gilroy, Paul. *There Ain't No Black in the Union Jack*. London: University of Chicago Press, 1991. First published in 1987 by Unwin Hyman Ltd.

————. "This Island Race." *New Statesman and Society*, 3.86 (2 February 1990) 30.

Godiwala, Dimple. *Alternatives Within the Mainstream: British Black and Asian Theatres*. Cambridge: Cambridge Scholars, 2006.

Goodman, Lizbeth. *Contemporary Feminist Theatre: To Each Her Own*. London and New York: Routledge, 1993.

Gordon, Paul. *Policing Immigration: Britain's Internal Controls*. London: Pluto Press, 1985.

Grene, Nicholas. *The Politics of Irish Drama: Plays in Context from Boucicault to Friel*. Cambridge: Cambridge University Press, 1999.

Grene, Nicholas, and Chris Morash, editors. *Irish Theatre on Tour: Irish Theatrical Diaspora Series (no. 1)*. Dublin: Carysfort Press, 2005.

Griffin, Gabriele. "Theatres of Difference: The Politics of 'Redistribution' and 'Recognition' in the Plays of Contemporary Black and Asian Women Playwrights in Britain," *Postcolonial Theatres Issue*, a special issue of *Feminist Review*, 84 (2006) 10–28.

————. *Contemporary Black and Asian Playwrights in Britain.* Cambridge: Cambridge University Press, 2003.

Griffiths, Trevor R., and Margaret Llewellyn-Jones, editors. *British and Irish Women Playwrights Since 1958.* Buckingham and Philadelphia: Open University Press, 1993.

Gupta, Akhil, and James Fergusen. "Beyond Culture: Space, Identity, and the Politics of Difference." *Cultural Anthropology,* (July 1992) 6–23.

Halbreich, Kathy. Exhibition Brochure, "No Place (Like Home)." Walker Art Center, 9 March-8 June 1997.

Hall, Stuart. *The Hard Road to Renewal: Thatcherism and the Crisis of the Left.* London: Verso, 1988.

Hall, Stuart, and Paul du Gay, editors. *Questions of Cultural Identity.* London: Sage Press, 1996.

Hall, Stuart, with Chas Critcher, Tony Jefferson, John Clark, and Brian Robert, *Policing the Crisis: 'Mugging,' The State, and Law and Order.* London: MacMillan, 1978.

Harding, Jeremy. *The Uninvited: Refugees at the Rich Man's Gate.* London: Profile Books with London Review of Books, 2000.

Harney, Stefano. *Nationalism and Identity: Culture and the Imagination in the Caribbean Diaspora.* London and New Jersey: Zed Books, 1996.

Harvie, Jen. *Staging the UK.* Manchester and New York: Manchester UP, 2005.

Hickman, Mary J. "Reconstructing Deconstructing 'Race': British Political Discourse about the Irish in Britain." *Ethnic and Racial Studies,* 21.2 (March 1998) 288–307.

Hickman, Mary J., and Bronwen Walter, *Discrimination and the Irish Community in Britain: A Report of Research Undertaken for the Commission for Racial Equality.* London: CRE, 1997.

Hill, Errol. *Shakespeare in Sable: A History of Black Shakespearean Actors.* Amherst: University of Massachusetts Press, 1984.

Hingorani, Dominic. *British Asian Theatre: Dramaturgy, Process, and Performance.* London: Palgrave MacMillan, 2010.

Hiro, Dilip. *Black British, White British: A History of Race Relations in Britain.* London: Eyre and Spottiswoode, 1971.

Holmes, Colin. *John Bull's Island: Immigration and British Society 1851–1971.* Basingstoke and London: MacMillan Education, 1988.

Husband, Charles, editor. *'Race' in Britain: Continuity and Change.* London: Hutchinson, 1982.

Itzin, Catherine. *Stages in the Revolution: Political Theatre in Britain since 1968.* London: Eyre Methuen, 1980.

Joseph, May Rosalind. *Nomadic Identities: The Performance of Citizenship.* Minneapolis, University of Minnesota Press, 1999.

Joseph, May Rosalind, and Jennifer Natalya Fink, editors. *Performing Hybridity.* Minneapolis: University of Minnesota Press, 1999.

Judt, Tony. *Postwar: A History of Europe Since 1945.* New York: The Penguin Press, 2005.

Kearney, Richard. *Postnationalist Ireland: Politics, Culture, Philosophy.* London and New York: Routledge, 1997.

————. *Transitions: Narratives in Modern Irish Culture.* Dublin: Wolfhound Press, 1987.

Kearney, Richard, editor. *Across the Frontiers: Ireland in the 1990's.* Dublin: Wolfhound Press, 1988.

————. *Migrations: The Irish at Home and Abroad.* Dublin: Wolfhound Press, 1989.

Keogh, Dermot. *Twentieth-Century Ireland: Nation and State.* New York: St. Martin's Press, 1995.

Khan, Naseem. *The Arts Britain Ignores.* London: Arts Council Report, 1976.

King, Barnaby. "Landscapes of Fact and Fiction: Asian Theatre Arts in Britain." in *New Theatre Quarterly* 16.1 (February 2000).

King, Bruce, editor. *Post-Colonial English Drama.* New York: St. Martin's Press, 1992.

Knight, Franklin W., editor. *Modern Caribbean History.* Chapel Hill and London: University of North Carolina Press, 1989.

Kobialka, Michal A., editor. *Of Borders and Thresholds: Theatre History, Practice and Theory.* Minneapolis: University of Minnesota Press, 1999.

Kureishi, Hanif. *My Beautiful Launderette and Other Writings.*London: Faber and Faber, 1996.

Lacey, Stephen. *British Realist Theatre: The New Wave in Its Context.* London and New York: Routledge, 1995.

Lay, Samantha. *British Social Realism: From Documentary to Brit Grit.* London: Wallflower Press, 2002.

Lazarus, Neil. *Nationalism and Cultural Practice in the Postcolonial World.* Cambridge: Cambridge University Press, 1999.

Lee, A. Robert. *Other Britain, Other British: Contemporary Multicultural Fiction.* London and East Haven, CT: Pluto Press, 1995.

Lemelle, Sydney, and Robin Kelley, editors. *Imagining Home: Class, Culture, and Nationalism in the African Diaspora.* London: Verso, 1994.

Lesser, Wendy. *A Director Calls: Stephen Daldry and the Theatre.* London: Faber and Faber, 1997.

Ley, Graham. "Theatre of Migration and the Search for a Multicultural Aesthetic: Twenty Years of Tara Arts." *New Theatre Quarterly,* 13:52.

Lindsey, Lydia. "Halting the Tide: Responses to West Indian Immigration to Britain." *The Journal of Caribbean History* 26.1 (1992) 62–95.

Little, Kenneth. *Racial Relations in English Society.* London: Oxford University Press, 1948.

Mac Laughlin, Jim. *Ireland: The Emigrant Nursery and the World Economy.* Cork: Cork University Press, 1994.

———. *Historical and Recent Irish Emigration.* London: University of North London Press, 1994.

MacInnes, Colin. *England, Half English.* London: Hogarth Press/Chatto and Windus, 1986. First published in 1961 by MacGibbon and Kee, Limited.

Massey, Doreen. *Space, Place, and Gender.* Minneapolis: University of Minnesota Press, 1994.

McClintock, Anne. *Imperial Leather: Race, Gender, and Sexuality in the Colonial Contest.* New York and London: Routledge, 1995.

McCulloch, Christopher. *Theater and Europe: 1957–95.* Exeter: Intellect Books, 1996.

McGrath, John. *A Good Night Out: Popular Theatre: Audience, Class, and Form.* London: Methuen Drama, 1981.

McRobbie, Angela. *Post Modernism and Popular Culture.* London and New York: Routledge, 1994.

Mead, Matthew. "Empire Windrush: Cultural Memory and Archival Disturbance." *Moveable Type,* 3 (2007).

Mercer, Kobena. *Welcome to the Jungle: New Positions in Black Cultural Studies.* London: Routledge, 1994.

Merriman, Nick, editor. *The Peopling of London: Fifteen Thousand Years of Settlement from Overseas.* London: Museum of London, 1993.

Messina, Anthony. "The Not So Silent Revolution: Postwar Migration to Western Europe." *World Politics,* 49.1 (1996) 130–154.

Mohanram, Radhika. *Black Body: Women, Colonialism, and Space.* Minneapolis and London: University of Minnesota Press, 1999.

Moore, Robert and Tina Wallace. *Slamming the Door: The Administration of Immigration Control.* London: Martin Robertson and Company, 1975.

Morley, David, and Kuan-Hsing Chen. *Stuart Hall: Critical Dialogues in Cultural Studies.* London and New York: Routledge, 1996.

Morrison, Toni. *Playing in the Dark.* New York: Vintage, 1993.

Murphy, Robert, editor. *British Cinema in the 90s.* London: BFI Publishing, 1999.

Murray, Christopher. *Twentieth Century Irish Drama: Mirror up to Nation.* Manchester and New York: Manchester University Press, 1997.

Okokon, Susan. *Black Londoners: 1880–1990.* Phoenix Mill: Sutton Publishing, 1998.

Olaniyan, Tejumola. *Scars of Conquest/Masks of Resistance: the invention of cultural identities in African, African-American and Caribbean drama.* Oxford: Oxford University Press, 1995.

Omotoso, Kole. *The Theatrical into Theatre: A Study of the Drama and Theatre of the English-Speaking Caribbean.* London: New Beacon Books, 1982.

O'Toole, Fintan. *The Ex-Isle of Erin.* Dublin: New Island Books, 1997.

———. *The Lie of the Land: Irish Identities.* London: Verso Books, 1998.

———. *Tom Murphy: The Politics of Magic.* Dublin and London: New Island and Nick Hern Books, 1984.

Panayi, Panikos. *The Impact of Immigration: A Documentary History of the Effects and Experiences of Immigrants in Britain Since 1945.* Manchester and New York: Manchester University Press, 1999.

Paul, Kathleen. *Whitewashing Britain.* Ithaca, NY: Cornell University Press, 1997.

Pettinger, Alasdair, editor. *Always Elsewhere: Travels of the Black Atlantic.* London and New York: Cassell, 1998.

Phillips, Mike. *London Crossings: A Biography of Black Britain.* London and New York: Continuum, 2001.

Phillips, Mike, and Trevor Phillips. *Windrush: The Irresistible Rise of Multi-Racial Britain.* London: HarperCollins Publishers, 1998.

Pines, Jim. *Black and White in Colour: Black People in British Television Since 1936.* London: BFI Publishing, 1992.

Portes, Alejandro, Carlos Dore-Cabral and Patricia Landolt, editors. *The Urban Caribbean: Transition to the New Global Economy.* Baltimore and London: Johns Hopkins University Press, 1997.

Procter, James. *Dwelling Places: Postwar Black British Writing.* Manchester: Manchester University Press, 2003.

———. *Writing Black Britain: 1948–1998.* Manchester: Manchester University Press, 2000.

Rabey, David Ian. *British and Irish Political Drama in the Twentieth Century.* London: MacMillan, 1986.

Radhakrishnan, Rajagopalan. *Diasporic Mediations: Between Home and Location.* Minneapolis: University of Minnesota Press, 1996.

Rees, Roland. *Fringe First: Pioneers of Fringe Theatre On Record.* London: Oberon Books, 1992.

Rich, Paul. *Race and Empire in British Politics.* Cambridge: Cambridge University Press, 1986.

Roberts, Philip. *The Royal Court Theatre and the Modern Stage.* Cambridge: Cambridge University Press, 1999.

Rollins, Ronald Gene. *Divided Ireland: Bifocal Vision in Modern Irish Drama.* Lanham, MD: University Press of America, 1985.

Rushdie, Salman. *Imaginary Homelands: Essays and Criticism 1981–1991.* London: Granta/Penguin Books, 1991.

Rybczynski, Witold. *Home: A Short History of an Idea.* New York: Viking Penguin, Inc., 1986.

Safia Mirza, Heidi, editor. *Black British Feminism: A Reader.* London: Routledge, 1997.

Said, Edward. "The Art of Displacement: Mona Hatoum's Logic of Irreconcilables." In the exhibition catalogue *The Entire World as a Foreign Land.* London: Tate Gallery Publishing, Ltd., 2000.

Sandhu, Sukhdev. *London Calling: How Black and Asian Writers Imagined a City.* London: Harper Collins, 2003.

Santhanam, Kausalya. "Transcending Alienness." *The Hindu* (Online Edition), 17 March 2002, Sunday Magazine section.

Scally, R. J. *The End of Hidden Ireland: Rebellion, Famine, and Emigration.* New York: Oxford University Press, 1996.

Schroeder, Patricia. *The Feminist Possibilities of Dramatic Realism.* Madison, NJ: Farleigh Dickinson University Press, 1996.

Scobie, Edward. *Black Brittania: A History of Blacks in Britain.* Chicago: Johnson Publishing Company, 1972.

Segal, Ronald. *The Black Diaspora.* London: Faber and Faber, 1995.

Selway, Jacob. "'English-Born Reputed Strangers': Birth and Descent in Seventeenth-Century London." *Journal of British Studies*, 44 (October 2005).

Shank, Theodore, editor. *Contemporary British Theatre.* New York: St. Martin's Press, 1994.

Sharpe, Jenny. *Allegories of Empire: The Figure of Woman in the Colonial Text.* Minneapolis and London: University of Minnesota Press, 1993.

Sierz, Aleks. *Rewriting the Nation: British Theatre Today.* London: Methuen Drama, 2011.

Shellard, Dominic. *British Theatre Since the War.*New Haven and London: Yale University Press, 1999.

Smith, Anna Marie. *New Right Discourse on Race and Sexuality.* London: MacMillan Press Ltd., 1992.

Smith, Susan J. "Immigration and nation-building in Canada and the United Kingdom." In Jan Penrose and Peter Jackson, editors, *Constructions of Race, Place and Nation.* Minneapolis: University of Minnesota Press, 1993.

Smith, T. E. *Commonwealth Migration: Flows and Policies.* London: MacMillan Press, Ltd, 1981.

Solomos, John. *Race and Racism in the UK.* London: Palgrave MacMillan, 2003. First published in 1989.

Stone, Judy S. J. *Theatre.* London and Basingstoke: Macmillan, 1994.

Studlar, Donley T. "British Public Opinion, Colour Issues, and Enoch Powell: A Longitudinal Analysis." *British Journal of Political Science*, 4.3 (July 1974) 371–381.

Tranter, N. L. *British Population in the Twentieth Century.* London: MacMillan Press, Ltd, 1996.

Verma, Jatinder. "'Braids' and Theatre Practice." Transcript of a talk given at the British Braids Conference at Brunel University, Twickenham Campus, 20 April 2001.

———. "Asian Arts in the 21st Century." Speech given at Waterman Arts Centre, 24 March 2003. Courtesy of Tara Arts Archive (28 June 2005).

———. "Are We Visible?" Talk given at Peshkar Conference, Oldham, November 13, 2001. Courtesy of Tara Arts Archive (28 June 2005).

Wambu, Onyekachi, editor. *Hurricane Hits England: An Anthology of Writing about Black Britain.* New York: Continuum, 2000.

Waters, Anita M. *Race, Class, and Political Symbols: Rastafari and Reggae in Jamaican Politics.* New Brunswick and London: Transaction Publishers, 1985.

Wiley, Catherine, and Fiona Barnes, editors. *Homemaking: Women Writers and the Politics and Poetics of Home.* New York and London: Garland Publishing, 1996.

Williams, Eric. *Capitalism and Slavery.* Chapel Hill: Russell Publishers, 1944. Reprinted by Oxford University Press in 1964.

Winder, Robert. *Bloody Foreigners: The Story of Immigration to Britain.* London: Abacus Books, 2005.

Wright, Nicholas, Chair. *Platform Papers: Playwrights (No. 8).* London: National Theatre, 1995.

Younge, Gary. *Who Are We—And Should It Matter in the 21st Century?* London: Viking Penguin, 2010.

Reviews/Reports/Interviews

The 1991 Census Report. London: Office of Population Censuses and Surveys, 1991.

Battersby, Eileen. Review of Tom Murphy's novel, *The Seduction of Morality. The Observer,* 19 June 1994.

Billington, Michael. "East Is best." Review of *East Is East, Guardian,* 25 November 1996.

———. "England People Very Nice." Review of *England People Very Nice, Guardian,* 11 February 2009.

Burnham, Edward. "A Terrifying Play: The Fighting Carneys." *The Times,* 12 September 1961, p. 14.

Carpenter, Sandy. "Black and British Temba Forges the Mainstream: An Interview with Alby James." *The Drama Review,* 34.1 (Spring 1990).

Coveney, Michael. "Cross-Racial Casting." *The Observer,* 28 February 1993.

Espiner, Mark. "What to Say about...England People Very Nice." *The Guardian,* 13 February 2009.

Haydon, Andrew. "*England People Very Nice* Ridicules Racial Stereotypes." *Guardian,* 18 February 2009.

Kennedy, Douglas. Review of *A Whistle in the Dark. New Statesman and Society,* 14 July 1989.

Khan, Rabina. "Letter: Why I've Withdrawn from National Debate." *Guardian,* 4 March 2009.

Morley, Sheridan. *International Herald-Tribune,* 19 July 1989.

Nightingale, Benedict. "Stranger in a Strange Land." *The Times,* 25 November 1996.

Roy, Amit. "Why There Is No Business like Curry Business," from the programme for *Balti Kings* (2000). Courtesy of Tamasha Theatre Company.

Spencer, Charles. "Rich Mix of Culture and Comedy." *The Daily Telegraph,* 25 November 1996.

———. "Painful but True." *The Daily Telegraph,* July 12, 1989.

Taylor, Paul. *The Independent,* 25 November, 1996.

Tynan, Kenneth. "Wolves at the Door." *The Observer,* 17 September, 1961.

Talawa Company Profile. "Mission Statement." Provided by Talawa Theatre Company, November 1999.

Personal interview with Nicolas Kent (Artistic Director, Tricycle Theatre) conducted 14 February, 2000.

Personal interviews with Mustapha Matura conducted during November 1999 and December 2000.

Personal interviews with Kristine Landon-Smith conducted during October 2009.

Personal interviews with Jatinder Verma conducted during June 2005, October 2006, April 2008, and via email in March 2009.

Program for *A Love Song For Ulster,* Tricycle Theatre, April 1993. Provided by Tricycle Theatre, 14 February 2000.

"Whose Theatre: The Sustained Theatre Consultation" (report of a study conducted by Arts Council England, 2005).

Index

A

Abbensetts, Michael, *Sweet Talk*, 30, 44, 50, 74
Abbey Theatre, Dublin, 58, 64
Abrams, Oscar, 31
Achebe, Chinua, 29
Act of Union, 22
Actors Unlimited, 34
Adams, Robert, 29
Africa: Asians migrating from, 24, 33–34; immigration from, 13, 21, 23; publishing authors from, 29. *See also* West Africa
African immigrants, stereotypes of, 41–42
Ahmad, Rukhsana, 34, 88
Alibhai-Brown, Yasmin, 33–35, 79–80, 97; *Imagining the New Britain*, 93; *Nowhere to Belong*, 93, 94
Almost Free Theatre, 40
Anderson, Lindsay, 2
Angles, 20
The Archers (radio series), 85
Arcola Theatre, 88
Arts Council, 31, 33, 95
Asian Cooperative Theatre, 34
Asian immigrants: marriage and family of, 50; stereotypes of, 41; theatrical treatments of, 57. *See also* South Asian immigrants
Asians, 9, 23–25
Asian women in theater, 81, 83–84, 88–89
Aston, Elaine, 91
Ayckbourn, Alan, *House & Garden*, 2

B

Bains, Harwant, *Blood*, 43–45, 50
Barnes, Fiona, 3, 7
Barn theater company, 86
Barry, Sebastian, 35, 81

Bayley, Clare, *The Container*, 19, 38
Bean, Richard, *England People Very Nice*, 17–18
Beaton, Norman, 31
Behan, Brendan: *The Hostage*, 57; *The Quare Fellow*, 57
Belgrade Theatre, Coventry, 78
Bennett, Alan, 1
Bhabha, Homi, 6, 54, 96
Bhattacharya, Sonali, *A Thin Red Line*, 88
Bhatti, Gurpreet Kaur: *AD2050*, 78; *Behud*, 78; *Behzti*, 70–71, 73, 76–78, 80
Bhuchar, Sudha, 34, 87, 88
The Big Life, 38
Birmingham Repertory Theatre, 34, 53, 57, 78
Black British, 8–9
Black British theater, 30–33, 36, 81, 83–87
Black Mime Theatre, 31, 32
Black Mime Theatre Women's Troop, 90
black people in England and Britain, 21, 29–32
Black Theatre Co-Operative, 32, 34, 84, 97
Black Theatre of Brixton, 31
Black women in theater, 87–88
Black Women's Theatre Group, 87
Black Women Writers project, 87
Blythe, Ernest, 64
Brahmachari, Sita, 88
Brenton, Howard, 89
Brewer, Mary, 91
Brewster, Yvonne, 32, 86–87, 92
Bridewell Theatre, London, 6
Britain: climate of, 43–45; demographics of, 12–13, 17, 19–23; history of immigration in, 12–23, 93; immigrants' knowledge and expectations of, 5, 23, 39–41, 54, 80; myth of cultural homogeneity in, 14–16, 19. *See also* national identity
British Asian theater, 23–24, 32–34
British Asian Theatre Archive, 36

X

POSTCOLONIAL STUDIES
Maria C. Zamora, *General Editor*

The recent global reality of both forced and voluntary migrations, massive transfers of population, and traveling and transplanted cultures is seen as part and parcel of the postindustrial, postmodern, postcolonial experience. The Postcolonial Studies series will explore the enormous variety and richness in postcolonial culture and transnational literatures.

The series aims to publish work which explores various facets of the legacy of colonialism including: imperialism, nationalism, representation and resistance, neocolonialism, diaspora, displacement and migratory identities, cultural hybridity, transculturation, translation, exile, geographical and metaphorical borderlands, transnational writing. This series does not define its attentions to any single place, region, or disciplinary approach, and we are interested in books informed by a variety of theoretical perspectives. While seeking the highest standards of scholarship, the Postcolonial Studies series is thus a broad forum for the interrogation of textual, cultural and political postcolonialisms.

The Postcolonial Studies series is committed to interdisciplinary and cross cultural scholarship. The series' scope is primarily in the Humanities and Social Sciences. For example, topics in history, literature, culture, philosophy, religion, visual arts, performing arts, language & linguistics, gender studies, ethnic studies, etc. would be suitable. The series welcomes both individually authored and collaboratively authored books and monographs as well as edited collections of essays. The series will publish manuscripts primarily in English (although secondary references in other languages are certainly acceptable). Page count should be one hundred and twenty pages minimum to two hundred and fifty pages maximum. Proposals from both emerging and established scholars are welcome.

For additional information about this series or for the submission of manuscripts, please contact:

Maria C. Zamora
c/o Acquisitions Department
Peter Lang Publishing
29 Broadway, 18th floor
New York, New York 10006

To order other books in this series, please contact our Customer Service Department:

(800) 770-LANG (within the U.S.)
(212) 647-7706 (outside the U.S.)
(212) 647-7707 FAX

Or browse online by series:
www.peterlang.com